Derby Dreams

How You Can Pursue the Dream to Own a Racehorse

By
Mary Lou Werner

Published by
Dark Horse Publishing Co.

Published by Dark Horse Publishing Co.
Rosemount, Minnesota

First Edition

First Printing • July 1995

Library of Congress Card Number: 95-92258

ISBN 0-9646449-0-8

Photo Credits: Paula Estlund Copyright © 1990

Illustration Credits: Jodi Reeb-Myers

Additional copies may be obtained by the order form
found at the back of this book.

Printed in the USA by

*M*ORRIS
PUBLISHING

3212 E. Hwy 30
Kearney, NE 68847
800-650-7888

To Jodi, my sister,
who supported me from the beginning
with my dream.

To So Long LeSueur, my first racehorse,
for making the dream come true,
and for changing my entire life.

And in loving memory to my mother, Alma,
whose last gift to me was Mr Toi Dancer,
who became my Derby Dream.

TO:
Bette
Dream Big!
Mary Lou Werner

ACKNOWLEDGMENTS

I wish to thank my sister, Jodi Reeb-Myers, for contributing her special artistic talents in drawing three of the illustrations in this book. The cover illustration was created by the artistic staff of Morris Publishing. Thanks also to Paula Estlund, equine photographer, for the photographic contribution on the title page of myself and my favorite racehorse, So Long LeSueur.

I wish to express special gratitude to my editor, Bette A. Voss, whose editorial suggestions showed remarkable sensitivity and depth of knowledge of the racing industry.

A special note of thanks to Janet Del Castillo, author of <u>Backyard Race Horse</u>. After reading her excellent book, her words have become an influence to me on the care and training of the racehorse. Informed ownership is the key.

Additionally, I'd like to acknowledge the unsung heroes of the backside — all of the trainers, jockeys, and grooms that I have been in contact with since 1989. They are the ones who really make the dream possible. I learned everything about owning a racehorse from them.

Lastly, I would like to thank my husband, Dana, for putting up with me during the past year while writing this book. He also contributed the illustration of the horse. Without his patience, understanding, moral support, and persistent urging to keep writing, this book would not be a reality today.

TABLE OF CONTENTS

Preface

Introduction

PREFACE

The first time I went to a race track was in 1986. It was Canterbury Downs in Minnesota. I went because my sales unit had won a top sales award and our prize was a day at the races. I didn't bet much that day, I didn't know how. But I liked the horses and I liked the excitement within the crowd.

I didn't go back to the track until the following year. My brother-in-law, Curt, had extra tickets and wanted me to attend the races with him and my sister, Rosie. That day I learned a little about handicapping and how to bet. I even cashed some winning tickets. I liked the races enough to ask a friend to join me the following weekend. I cashed more tickets and became hooked on the horses. I enjoyed going out to the track and started going by myself.

Over the next year, I became a serious handicapper who was avid to learn everything and anything about horse racing. I became a regular at the walking ring, watching the grooms, trainers, and owners with their horses. As I leaned over the white picket fence separating me from them, something began to burn within me.

That burning caught on fire in 1988. I realized I was no longer content to just bet on the horses, I wanted to become a part of the action and own a horse. I went to my first horse auction that year and had to sit on my hands to prevent me from bidding on those beautiful animals. I attended horse seminars and talked to other owners. There were no books written about owning a racehorse, and I had no idea how much it would cost or anything about the racing business. I did realize, however, that it was expensive. I knew I didn't have that kind of money and had no idea there were partnerships out there.

In November of 1988, I went to Churchill Downs to attend the Breeders' Cup. It was a dream come true for me. It was the year that Personal Ensign retired undefeated and Alysheba won the Classic and broke John Henry's leading money earned record. But something else happened. I went to the historical Kentucky Derby Museum on the grounds of Churchill Downs. This exhibition portrays the finest horses that ever lived and the grand finale was a film showing a day in the life of a racehorse. The film was shown on a screen that surrounded the audience. It took me onto the backside, through a morning gallop, onto a race, and into the winner's circle. I found out that a lot of people form partnerships to be able to afford a horse. I had tears running down my face as I watched it. I knew then and there I wanted to pursue the dream to own a racehorse, and I could afford only a partnership.

When I returned home, I diligently searched the want ads of every newspaper looking for a partnership. Just when I was ready to give up hope, "the ad" appeared just after Christmas. The price was right, the time was right, and the horse was right. In December of 1988, I joined a partnership in a yearling named So Long LeSueur, and the dream began.

Along with myself, there were two other partners who owned So Long. We raced him 2 1/2 years, and he won two races. I spent every evening, every weekend, and every race with him. He became my best friend and I learned about the backside, training, and disappointment with injuries. This gelding changed my life and owning him has been one of the greatest things that has ever happened to me. At the age of four, a gate injury forced his early retirement. I bought out the other partners and kept him. He is currently retired and living a life of luxury at a deluxe boarding stable where I spend my time with him. He is turned out daily in a paddock where he feels the wind in his mane and the rapture of running free.

One year after joining my first partnership, I joined a second partnership. The horse was a filly named Keepaneyeoutforme. She was a one-eyed horse with a big heart and was my first major winner giving me a profit. I lost her when she was claimed in a race in 1990 .

Partnerships were doing well for me and I was riding on a high, so I joined a third partnership in 1991. The horse was a flashy, red chestnut by the name of Northern Islands. He was an allowance horse who liked to come from behind way off the pace in long distance races. I joined the partnership with my fiancee, Dana, who I introduced to the world of racing. Northern Islands is still racing for us today.

After getting married in 1991, Dana and I decided we could afford a horse on our own and in 1992, Paige Me First joined our stable. Shortly after that, we formed a joint venture partnership with two members of my family. After being in three partnerships, I finally got first-hand experience at managing my own partnership. In 1993, we dissolved the joint venture and my husband and I continued to race her. While she was prepping for a big stakes race in Nebraska, we discovered bone chips in both front legs. One week away from the biggest race of her career, and we had to retire her. She had two wins and won $10,000 for us. Once we retired her, we decided to become breeders and make her our foundation broodmare. She delivered her first foal, a colt, in April 1995. It's amazing how things happen starting out with just one horse!

After Paige's retirement, we purchased a yearling, a gelding by the name of Mr Toi Dancer. Owning him was a dream for me. Three years earlier, I had wanted to buy his sister, Terrible Toi. But she was sold before I could purchase her. She went on to break her maiden at the age of two by 14 lengths and was stakes placed in two races. The following year her half-brother, Little Toi Soldier, won two stakes races in Illinois. Now I own Mr Toi Dancer, full brother to Terrible Toi, and he became my first real hope for a "derby" horse. He won his first race at the age of three and has run in the Turf Paradise Derby. Barring any injuries or bad racing luck, he has many more prospects ahead. With him, hope springs eternal. For tomorrow we may get that Derby win.

There are now many associations available to help educate you on becoming a horse owner, but few books written for a new owner. When I started out in the business, there was nothing written about ownership. I had to learn it from the ground up, and I made many mistakes, some of them costly. The horses and the industry have given me so much that I wish to give something back to it. I see the need for a book on ownership and want to fulfill that need. My wish is to educate and encourage all of you who have the desire to own a racehorse to spread your wings and try it. This book will help you get started. If you choose to own a racehorse, your life will never be the same. Because of the variety of partnerships and types of ownerships, you can start at whatever level you can afford and work your way up. Racehorse ownership can be affordable to anyone who wants to pursue the dream of owning one.

The road has not always been easy for me and may not be for you. There will be ups and downs. I have made many mistakes, had poor trainers and good trainers. I've stood in the winner's circle with each of my horses, and I've stood in each of their stalls when they were sick or injured and had to miss a race. When things were going well, I stood on top of the world; when things were going bad, I sunk to the lowest depths of despair. But I never gave up. Having experienced low periods, it made the highs much sweeter and more treasured. There are no guarantees in horse racing. But the one thing that kept me going in all those times, was the love and thrill of owning that horse no matter where he/she ran in a race. If you love horses and love horse racing, you have to love them no matter what class they are or where they run. I've been lucky. Every horse I have owned has made it to the track and has won one or more races. And I have cherished every one of them. This book is a product of what I have learned and what has been successful for me. My success has been measured in enjoyment rather than dollars. Because if you are in this business for only the money, you will be sadly disappointed. Owning a racehorse is an investment in the love of the sport, not the profit. I am an average owner who can't afford the top horses that sell at Keeneland. Yet, I've been successful with the horses I could afford and enjoyed them all just the same.

Derby Dreams is full of hope in finding the "big horse." But, if at first you don't succeed; try, try again. But most importantly, enjoy your racehorse ownership experience today, for tomorrow it may be gone. Horses are fragile and must be taken care of properly. The following poem can best describe enjoying "today." I found this poem in my mother's purse. As she was dying from cancer, she carried it with her wherever she went to remind her of how important it was to enjoy "today." The poem was written on a scrap of paper; the author is unknown, and it goes like this;

"Put yesterday behind you, it's gone and won't come back. And we cannot see ahead far down tomorrow's track. Enjoy the fleeting moments that come just for today. The sweet song of a bluebird, the morning sun's first ray. A warm and loving handclasp, welcome letters in the mail, a bunch of fragrant violets, rain splashing in a pail. Each day has something special, some joy or souvenir. It might be gone tomorrow, so enjoy it while it's here."

If you make mistakes, put them behind you for you won't make them again. Each horse is something special, a joy to be with; each racing day and morning on the backside is a souvenir. If you are fortunate to own a winning horse, treasure him, something unexpected may happen and he might be gone tomorrow. So truly enjoy him while he's here!

During my life, I have travelled many places, met many people, seen many things. But of all the places my travels have led, the happiest of times have been with my thoroughbreds!

M.L. Werner

INTRODUCTION

Horse racing is known as the "Sport of Kings" and many think it is only a sport enjoyed by the wealthy. The growth and availability of partnerships has made the "Sport of Kings" ownership affordable to a large number of people.

Have you ever dreamed of owning a racehorse, but didn't know where to begin? Have you ever dreamed of standing in the winner's circle, but wondered how you could pick out a potential winner? Have you ever dreamed of being in a derby, but thought you could never afford to enter one? This is where racehorse ownership begins - with dreams, derby dreams.

But the dream is only the beginning. Before you stand in the winner's circle, you must select the level of ownership you can afford, purchase a horse with potential running ability, and hire a trainer to get you there. If you are fortunate to find that "Derby Horse," you might have to form a partnership to make it affordable.

The purpose of this book is to introduce you to the variety of ownerships, differences in partnerships, how to select a racehorse, and hire a trainer. You will also learn about the expenses involved in owning a racehorse, the people and officials within the racing business, and a chance to evaluate how much you can afford to spend.

The information contained in this book comes from years of real-life experience owning, breeding, and racing horses. This experience was gained by starting out small in a partnership, learning to form partnerships, and working up to being a sole proprietor and breeder. It can be done. Dreams can come true. The knowledge and information gained from this book, can help you make a start into owning a racehorse. The chapters will explore some of the criteria that can help make this decision more profitable and rewarding while helping you determine how much you can afford. Nothing spoils a dream quicker than investing more than you can afford.

We are all dreaming of the big horse, a "Derby Horse." While the ultimate goal is to have a horse in the "Kentucky Derby," there are many hundreds of smaller "derbies" you can aim for along the way. When you step into the winner's circle of any race, it will be the high of a lifetime. Nothing can compare to the joy of winning a race and standing in the winner's circle. It's like nothing you've ever done before.

Derby Dreams—the key to happiness is having dreams, the key to success is making dreams come true. The future belongs to those who believe in their dreams.

1

Types of Ownership

The first step in owning a racehorse is to decide on the type of ownership you want to have. There are many forms of ownership available today and each form brings with it a different degree of expense, complexity, advantages, and disadvantages. It is important that you consider what you want to get out of ownership and how much you can afford to spend on it.

What kind of a person are you? How involved do you want to be in the handling of the horse? Will you be in it for fun and enjoyment or a serious business venture? How much can you afford to spend or lose? Do you want immediate action now or do you want to invest in a young horse and watch it grow and develop? Do you want to share the risk with someone or go it alone? Do you need to learn the basics of the business of racing?

Owning a racehorse can be a fun and rewarding venture. It is filled with risk, expenses, and the unknown. It is important to explore the various forms of ownership. Look carefully at the advantages and disadvantages of each one. After you have determined what you want out of owning a racehorse and how much you can afford to spend, you will find the type of ownership with which you can be comfortable.

Sole Proprietor

This is the simplest form of business organization. Apart from you, the owner, the business has no existence.

ADVANTAGES. Being the sole proprietor means you will be able to make all the decisions with the trainer regarding the horse. There will be no other partners to consult with on issues of buying, selling, or racing the horse. You will be the "sole" person deciding how to run your business. You will be able to run the horse under your own colors (jockey silks). The business liabilities are also your personal liabilities. The proprietary interest ends when you die or when you sell the horse.

DISADVANTAGES. As sole proprietor, you undertake responsibility for all the bills and liabilities. You will be responsible for all the risks of the business, win or lose. However, once that purse money starts pouring in, it is yours and does not have to be shared with partners. For the first-time owner, sole proprietor can be tough to get started. This form of ownership takes a great deal of money and, if you are new to the business, you will need a mentor who has the knowledge and experience that you have not yet acquired.

Partnerships

A partnership is the relationship existing between two or more persons. Each person contributes their share of money toward the liabilities and each expect to share in the profits and losses of the partnership. Partnerships are a great way to introduce yourself to racing. You will learn a lot at a level of risk you can afford. Owning a percentage in a horse becomes affordable to most people. Partnerships are a great way to start in the racing business.

ADVANTAGES. The partnership is operated and controlled by a written or oral partnership agreement. Each partner's share of income, expenses, and liability is determined by the percentage owned. The minimum percentage required to be a licensed partner is only 5%. However, percentages can be as high as you can comfortably afford to pay.

All partners have voting privileges. They have the right to make decisions and voice opinions regarding the horse. New owners can enter a partnership with a modest investment and gain valuable experience and education about the business while spreading the risk with others. From here, many partners go on and take the next step and become a sole proprietor.

Through partnerships you will have the enjoyment of seeing that horse grow up and race. You can have fun and be in on the action without having the responsibility of running the entire business. You will also meet many people and make new friends.

DISADVANTAGES. You will not have a full say in the running of the horse and the business. Other partners may vote your idea down, majority rules. The horse may run in the colors of the partner who owns the largest percentage. If the trainer is one of the majority partners, you may have less say in racing matters. Except for a limited partner (see Limited Partnerships) each individual partner can be held liable for the actions of the other partners.

There are two varieties of partnerships, limited and general. There is a difference between the two which is explained in the next section.

GENERAL PARTNERSHIPS. This partnership is operated under the principles stated above. General partnerships can range from relatively simple methods of doing business to very complicated ones. All expenses, liabilities, and income are shared by all partners based on the percentage owned. Unexpected expenses may occur throughout the racing season (e.g., horse is injured, etc.) and must be shared by all partners. As stated earlier, each individual partner can be held liable for the actions of the other partners.

A general partnership is usually run by a managing partner who may or may not own the largest percentage. The managing partner usually conducts business with the trainer and keeps the records, receives the bills, and makes the payments. All other partners give their input, ideas, and opinions to the managing partner.

A general partnership can be dissolved in several ways. One partner can buy out another who wishes to get out. Another way is to dissolve the entire partnership and sell the assets (horses). For tax purposes, a general partnership usually files one income tax return and allows partners to claim losses or gains the same year that they occur, as long as you can prove active involvement in business decisions.

LIMITED PARTNERSHIPS. A limited partnership is similar to a regular partnership EXCEPT for the following. Each limited partner contributes their share of money toward expenses and liability to a managing partner. Some limited partnerships calculate a yearly total. The limited partner may pay their percentage for the year ahead of time. If any additional expenses occur during the year, they do not have to pay any additional amount. They know upfront what amount they are liable for that year.

Limited partners usually DO NOT have voting privileges or the right to make decisions. This right is reserved for the managing partner only. Limited partners also have limited liability for the actions of the other partners. This is a more passive form of a partnership. Because of the passive nature of this partnership, income tax losses/gains can be affected. If taxes are an important consideration to you, a tax accountant should be consulted before signing any partnership agreements.

Limited partnerships usually require a modest investment, and accomplishments of the horses also tend to be a bit more modest. Dissolving a limited partnership is the same as a general partnership.

HOW CAN I LOCATE A PARTNERSHIP? There are several ways you can locate people who may be looking for new partners. Many partnerships advertise in the horse section of major newspapers and trade journals. If you don't see any ads, place one of your own. Join local or national horse racing/breeding associations. (See appendix.) Attend their events and get to meet and know other owners, breeders, and trainers. Consult with other owners. Visit breeding farms and training centers. They are all business people and will welcome potential customers. Call the Racing Secretary at your local track or track of interest and ask for recommendations of people you can talk to. Observe trainers in the saddling paddock and call the trainers who appeal to you. Meet with them for coffee on the Backside. Consult with the Bloodstock Agents or start your own partnership.

Syndicate

A syndicate is the public sale of the multiple interest in a horse.

ADVANTAGES. A syndicate usually provides for assessments of the shareholders (owners) to cover the expenses of maintaining and racing the horse. You are responsible only for your pro rata share of the total expenses. If another owner defaults on his agreement to contribute towards the costs, you are not responsible for the shortfall.

DISADVANTAGES. You will have limited decision-making ability. If a judgement is entered against the entire syndicate, each owner could be found jointly and severally liable for any damages awarded. You can protect yourself by making a provision in the contract stating that the syndicate members will be only severally liable for any damages resulting from a breach of the contract, and that their liability will be limited to their pro rata interests in the horse. It is suggested you obtain legal and tax assistance before using the syndicate form of doing business.

Joint Venture (Co-Ownership)

A commercial undertaking by two or more persons, differing from a partnership in that it relates to the completion of a single project, is considered a joint venture or co-ownership. Its duration is limited to the period in which the project is carried on. The termination is usually clearly defined in a written agreement.

ADVANTAGES. Like a general partnership, each partner shares expenses, liabilities, and income based on percentage owned. The joint venture agreement will have a definite starting and ending date with a renewal clause. The partners may be able to report their income, deductions, and losses on their personal income tax.

DISADVANTAGES. A managing partner will make all of the major decisions. At the end of the agreement, if one partners wants to renew the joint venture but the others do not, that partner must buy out the others partners or dissolve it.

Corporations

A corporation is a legal entity operating under a grant of authority from a state in the form of articles of incorporation or a charter.

REGULAR CORPORATION. The basic attributes of a corporation are: an exclusive name, continued existence within the limits of its articles of incorporation, paid-in capital represented by transferable shares, limited liability for debts and obligations beyond amount of full-paid capital stock, and centralization of management. Forming a corporation involves a transfer of either money, property, or both in exchange for capital stock. This is a business entity that is seldom used in horse racing.

SUBCHAPTER S CORPORATION. This is a corporation that has chosen to be generally exempt from federal income tax. There is little flexibility in allocating income and losses among shareholders. A corporation can become a subchapter S corporation if: (1) it meets the requirements of subchapter S corporation status by having only one class of stock, has no more than 35 shareholders, and all shareholders must be citizens or residents of the United States; (2) all its shareholders consent to subchapter S corporation status; and (3) it uses a permitted tax year which is a calendar year.

A subchapter S corporation can substitute for your partnership or sole proprietorship and can limit your financial/legal liability. A subchapter S corporation may help overcome the hobby loss rules. Such a corporation is formed under state law. Subchapter S corporations are different from other types of corporations: (1) subchapter S corporations generally do not pay income tax from normal business profits. If there are losses, the losses flow through to the shareholders in proportion to their percentages of ownership; (2) the owners pay income tax on their pro rata shares by percentage owned; (3) the number of shareholders are limited to 35; and (4) its tax year must end on December 31.

This can be a flexible type of business entity. However, you should consult with a tax advisor to make sure you are observing the tax laws properly.

Limited Liability Companies

In recent years, a new form of doing business became available. This new entity is designated as Limited Liability Companies (LCCs). In 1988 an IRS ruling confirmed that an LCC would be taxed as a partnership. An LCC has the corporate characteristic of shielding its members from liability for debts, obligations, or liabilities--at least for the amount of a member's capital contribution. The LCC is not subject to Federal taxes and all Federal taxes pass through to its owners or members.

The LCC has the following characteristics: (1) the LCC entity is discontinued upon the death of a member, bankruptcy, or a date specified from formation; (2) management is decentralized to all or most of the members; and (3) a member's interest is not freely transferable as is shareholder's stock in a corporation.

The owners of an LCC are either members or transferees rather than partners, limited partners, or shareholders. Members can be an individual or an entity. The LCC formation is similar to that of a corporation except Articles of Organization are filed along with an operating agreement.

Leasing

If you don't care to purchase a horse--lease it! Leasing can be done either as a sole proprietor or a partnership. Each individual or partner agrees to lease a horse from the owner for a specified period of time. During this lease period, each person shares the income, expenses, and liability of the horse including maintenance until the lease expires. Each lease agreement is governed by the business entity chosen and the terms agreed upon. Some leases contain clauses for renewal of the lease at the expiration, or contain an option to buy at the expiration of the lease.

Contracts and Agreements

Partnerships may be formed by a simple handshake, a verbal agreement, or can be very detailed in a written contract. Corporations and syndicates will contain written contracts and agreements. Remember, no matter what business entity you are entering into, it is always a good idea to get it in writing. Consult a lawyer before drawing up or signing any papers with which you are not familiar.

Taxes

If your horse activities are conducted in a business-like manner with the intention of making a profit, there may be expenses you can deduct from your other income.

BUSINESS PLAN. When starting a business entity for horse racing, develop a written business plan showing how you intend to make the operation profitable. It should establish your goals and provide a comparison to the future results of your operation. The plan should include, but not be limited to: (1) your expertise in the horse business and/or advisors used; (2) your expectation of appreciation in business assets; (3) any success in similar activities; (4) definition of your goals; (5) calculation of the funds you have available to reach those goals; (6) development of short-range and long-range plans; (7) putting your ideas on paper; (8) listing of possible roadblocks to your success and strategies to overcome them; and (9) preparation of cash flow projections and profit and loss projections.

COMPLETE RECORDS. You will need to maintain complete and accurate books and records on your business activities. All good business records are supported by sales slips, invoices, canceled checks, paid bills, contracts, and other documents.

BUSINESSLIKE MANNER In order to be eligible to deduct losses on your income tax, your horse business must be conducted in a "businesslike" manner. To become "businesslike" you will need to maintain complete and accurate books and records; the activity should be carried on in a similar manner to other profitable activities; demonstrate a change in methods in activities that are unprofitable; display adoption of new techniques; and show the abandonment of unprofitable methods. Tax laws are a consideration for ownership—but should not be an overriding concern. You should be more concerned about getting value for your dollar and then enjoy it.

Because of the complex tax laws in the horse industry, it is best to seek the advice of an accountant with horse taxation ownership/partnership experience.

Educate Yourself

The best way to begin a new venture is to read, read, read. What you lack in experience can be gained in educating yourself in the horse business. Read books (see bibliography), join horse associations (see appendix), subscribe to industry magazines such as <u>The Blood Horse</u> and <u>The Thoroughbred Times</u>, attend seminars, and request statistics from The Jockey Club or Bloodstock Research Information on bloodlines and trainers.

Once you have entered the horse business, the education will be ongoing. You will never stop learning. Every year and with every horse with every race, you will learn something new. An informed, educated owner is an asset to the racing industry.

2

How to Select/Buy a Horse

The goal of virtually every horse owner is to one day find himself (or herself) in the winner's circle. Before you can get to the winner's circle, you must select a horse that is capable of getting you there. It has been said that the cheapest part you will pay is the purchase price of the horse. The training and maintenance of a horse will probably cost more than the purchase price.

There are two very important selections you must make in owning a racehorse. One is the horse, the other is the trainer. Good horses will cost about the same to train and maintain as "cheap" horses. Give yourself the best running chance by selecting the best horse that you can afford. Selecting a good running horse begins with conformation.

Conformation

Good conformation is important for athletic ability. Horses with good conformation are more likely to stay sound and withstand the stresses of training. When evaluating a horse, give your attention to the overall appearance. The horse should appear to be well-balanced with no obvious faults. A horse with good conformation usually has a "presence." Look for a horse with an intelligent, kind eye and large nostrils.

When he moves, it should be fluid and graceful. The following is not all inclusive, but contains some basic guidelines to help get you started in selecting a horse. The first step in learning conformation is to understand the terms used to identify the body parts of a horse. (See Figure 1.)

HEAD AND NECK. The horse's head should be proportionate to his size because the head helps maintain balance. A good length of neck allows freer movement for best balance in his exertions. The face should not be too narrow. A narrow face may interfere with flow of air when breathing hard, because of narrow nasal bones.

CHEST AND BODY. Body and leg conformation must be compatible. A long-bodied horse should be long-legged. A short-bodied horse must have shorter legs or he may overreach when he moves. The horse should have a deep heart girth. This will give him a lot of room for the lungs to expand. The horse should not be too narrow in the chest or his front legs may be too close together. There should be sufficient width between the front legs.

SHOULDER. The withers should be well-defined and of moderate height. Withers provide an anchor for the muscles that attach the shoulder blades to the body and assist in the movement of the front legs. Good withers and sloping shoulders usually go together.

QUARTERS. The croup (point where the pelvis meets the highest point of the hindquarters) should be well-rounded and surrounded by muscle.

FEET AND LEGS. The most important aspects of a horse's overall makeup are the feet and legs. The horse should have a good way of traveling, moving straight and clean. The feet should be well-shaped and of size in proportion to the size of the horse. If the feet are too small the horse won't hold up under strenuous training. If the feet are too large the horse may be clumsy. Legs that are calf knee, buck knee, tied-in knee, or cut-in at the knee will also cause the horse problems. (See Figure 4).

FRONT LEGS. The front legs should be well-balanced and straight. Toes should point directly to the front and the feet should be exactly the same distance apart as the distance between the forearms where they come out of the chest. Front legs that are too straight, base narrow, pigeon-toed, or splay-footed will cause the horse to be hard on himself in running. Horses with these leg defects usually will have problems and may cause higher veterinarian costs as well. (See Figure 2.)

BASE-WIDE, NARROW. Front legs should be perfectly straight when viewed from the front or the side. Base-narrow conformation puts the horse's feet too close together. Base-narrow conformation is often accompanied by pigeon toes (pointing inward), which puts strains on pastern and fetlock joints. (See Figure 2.)

HINDQUARTERS. The hindquarters of a horse, in comparison to the back legs, should not be too straight, "out in the country," or sickle-hocked. An illustration of a good hindquarters is found at the end of this chapter. Hindquarters that have these defects will cause the horse to have stifle problems. (See Figure 3.)

Public Auctions

Horses are usually purchased at a sale or public auction. Sale catalogs are issued several weeks before the sale giving you an opportunity to analyze the bloodlines of the horses. The sales may be at a national level in Kentucky or can be conducted by a state owner's and breeder's association.

READ THE SALES CATALOG. The sales catalog is one of the best sources of information available, and it is important to know how to read it. It contains information on terms and conditions of the sale, foal's gender, date-of-birth, color, several generations of pedigree, biography of the family's racing, and stakes engagements.

However, be aware that catalogs are essentially promotional pieces meant to accentuate the positive and eliminate the negative. A horse's pedigree will give you at least an idea of what you might expect from him or her in the future. It is wise to consult with an equine advisor or reputable bloodstock expert when going to a sale.

In reading a sales catalog, it is important to look for horses who have dams and sires who have run successfully. Then look for a dam who has had offspring who have run successfully. This is a good indication that this foal may be a runner.

Sales catalogs can be mailed out in advance. To get on a mailing list, you will need to contact a national sales association, such as Fasig-Tipton or Keeneland, or a local owner's and breeder's association. (See appendix.)

MEET THE CONSIGNORS. The sales consignors make the horses available for viewing before each sale. The consignor's goals are to have the horses show, handle, and look the best they can. They are available for questions. Horses are usually sold with no guarantees. If you are concerned about the medical health of a horse, you can hire a veterinarian to check the horse prior to the sale. The veterinarian can do a full set of X-rays and a scope examination. However, this exam could cost several hundred dollars.

VIEWING PROSPECTIVE HORSES. It is highly recommended that you view the horse(s) before they step into the sales ring. The consignors will be more than happy to take

their horses out of the stalls and walk them for you to view
their conformation.

PAYMENT OF ACCOUNT. Most sales will state the requirements for payment of account in the sales catalog. Generally, the settlement of account must be made within 30
minutes of the conclusion of the sale for the full purchase
price. The horse becomes yours at the fall of the auctioneer's
hammer. Settlement is usually to be made in the form of U.S.
Currency (cash), certified check, traveler's check, or AP-
PROVED check, unless prior credit has been approved. Credit
may be established by presentation of a "Letter of Credit" or
approval of "Request for Credit." Purchasers to whom credit
is extended shall pay in full for their purchases within five
days of the sale. A request for credit should be presented to
the sales agency at least one week PRIOR to the sale so the
request can be verified and credit approved.

SHIPPING THE HORSE HOME. Once a horse has been
purchased at a sale, you will have 12-24 hours to move it
from the sales grounds. You will need to make arrangements
with a vanning company to provide this service if you do
not own a horse trailer. The average charge for commercial
vanning is between 30-50 cents per mile. It is also a good
idea to make arrangements for a stall or stalls at a stable or
training center before going to the sale.

Private Sales

BREEDING FARMS. Instead of purchasing a horse
through public auction you may wish to purchase a horse
directly from a breeding farm. There can be many advantages
to this method. You will be able to get to know the breeder
and how they run their operation. You can watch their
foals develop.

Start by getting a list of local breeders from an owner's and breeder's association. Call and introduce yourself and make an appointment to visit their farm. Once there, get information about the success of earlier foal crops and find out the bloodlines of the foals now on the ground. Study your bloodlines and if interested in a particular foal, visit often to watch its growth and development. Look for the "alpha" of a foal crop. The alpha is the strong, dominant foal who is the leader of a group of foals.

Most breeding farms will want to sell a horse when it is a weanling or a yearling. To purchase the horse from the farm, you will need to make an offer for the horse before it goes to public auction. Purchasing a young horse will mean you will have to provide care and maintenance on it until it becomes a two-year-old. If you don't want to wait several years to see the horse race, you might want to consider another option - claiming a horse from the track.

Claiming a Horse

INSTANT ACTION. Throughout the country race tracks run a large number of races called claiming races. These races are run on a daily basis and the claiming price can range anywhere from $2,500 to $50,000 or greater. A claiming race is written to enable a trainer to enter a horse at a competition level. Any horse entered in a claiming race is subject to be claimed for its entered price by any other trainer or licensed owner. If you want to claim a horse, you will need to apply for a temporary claiming license or a claiming authorization from the stewards. For a new owner who wants instant action, claiming a horse may be the answer. Instead of buying a yearling and waiting a year or more, a claimed horse is ready to race without waiting.

Breeding Your Own Horse

One of the ultimate thrills in owning a racehorse is breeding, raising, and racing your own horse. The excitement of leading your homebred into the winner's circle can be the thrill of a lifetime.

PURCHASE/LEASE BROODMARE. The initial investment in breeding will be to purchase a broodmare at a public breeding auction. If you have limited funds you may wish to lease a broodmare to see how she produces. Unless you own a farm, you will need to board your mare at a farm that can provide care for broodmares and their foals. Some of the risks you may encounter are: (1) will the mare settle and become pregnant; (2) will she deliver a foal or does she have complicated deliveries requiring additional expenses; and (3) will she produce a healthy, well-conformed foal. Once the foal is born on the ground, you will have at least two years of nothing but bills until the horse begins its racing career at the age of two. If you decide to sell the foal, the selling price will be determined by its conformation and the bloodline of its stallion as well as the produce record of the mare. Choosing an appropriate stallion for your mare is a very important decision.

SELECT A STALLION. Educate and familiarize yourself with the bloodlines of stallions. Look at past breeding and "nicking" patterns of these stallions with the bloodline of your mare. Research the racing careers of the foals of these matings. Were they successful or did they fail to make it to the track? Stallion progeny and broodmare produce reports are available from agencies such as Bloodstock Research. Give your foal the best chance of being a winner by breeding a good mare to a good stallion with a proven track record. Breeding to a stallion just because he's cheap could cost you more in the end if the foal can't race.

Once you have chosen that "perfect" stallion for your mare, seek out the farm where the stallion stands. They will give you the price of the stallion's service (no it's not free) and whether his "book" is still open. Stallions breed to a limited number of mares each year. You will need to know when they want the mare there, how much they charge per day for broodmare care, and any additional charges for ultra-sound and veterinarian expenses. There will also be shipping costs to and from the location of the stallion to your farm or boarding facility. In choosing a stallion you may wish to consult with a bloodstock agent.

You may also be able to purchase a "season" to a stallion at a stallion service auction. Usually, you will be able to purchase the season at a reduced price than the price for which the stallion currently stands. Some stallion service auctions will sponsor stakes races for the progeny of the stallions sold at that auction as an incentive to purchase the season.

Breeding your own horse takes time and patience. You will have the enjoyment of having planned the mating, watched the birth, saw the foal develop and mature into a racehorse. This alone may give you a satisfaction and excitement before you make it to the winner's circle. Whether buying or breeding, you must choose which suits your goals and objectives best.

FOAL-SHARING. Another option available for those who wish to breed their own horse, is a foal-sharing agreement with someone else. Foal-sharing is an agreement between a mare owner and a stallion season owner or purchaser whereby both parties co-own the resulting foal.

Even though both parties co-own the foal, the percentage owned can be negotiable. The expenses of board and maintenance of the mare remain the responsibility of the respective owner. This includes decisions relating to where the mare is kept. All foal-sharing agreements should be done through a written contract. Some important points to address in the contract are: (1) who will be in charge of the daily care of the foal, (2) the attending veterinarian, (3) the percentages of ownership in the foal, (4) who will be responsible for the foal's expenses, (5) where the mare/foal are to be kept, and (6) either distribution of sales proceeds or the decision to keep the foal to race.

Before making the decision to get into a foal-sharing agreement, decide if you will be able to work with the other party involved. The two of you will be working close together for 2-3 years sharing the potential racing prospect as well as sharing any problems that may arise. If you do not want to start breeding a foal on your own, foal-sharing may be the way for you to get a start into the racing business.

Bloodstock Agents

If you would like expert help in buying or breeding a horse, bloodstock agents are available to help you. A bloodstock agent will do the work of reading the sales catalog and checking out the conformation of the horses. They will then advise you which horse or horses are best and worth bidding on within your price range. However, there is a charge for this service which is usually 5% of the purchase price of the horse, if you do buy one. For breeding assistance, percentages will vary. Bloodstock agents are licensed by each state. Before choosing one, be sure and check with the state's racing commission office to get a list of the agents and their background.

Age of a Horse

In purchasing a horse, you might want to consider the age of the horse. Do you want a weanling, yearling, or a two-year-old in training? If you purchase a younger horse, you will have more expenses and it will take longer to get to the track. But a weanling may go for a cheaper price than if you want until it is one or two years old. Remember, no matter in what month the horse was born, all horses are considered to have a "birthday" on January 1 of each year. This is important if you want to race a two-year-old. If you purchase a horse born in May, it may not be as developed or mature as a horse born in February. Once they turn three, this difference usually disappears.

WEANLING. A weanling is a foal after it has been weaned from its dam and before it becomes a yearling on January 1. The benefit of purchasing a weanling is that you may get it at a reduced cost than waiting until it is a yearling. The disadvantage is that you will have an additional year of care and maintenance before you can begin breaking and training.

YEARLING. A yearling is a horse that is considered to be one year old because of the January 1 birthday rule. In reality, the horse is somewhere between a weanling and its true first birthday. The majority of public auctions are yearling sales. These sales will begin in the summer months and continue through November of each year. The "select" sales will contain the horses with the better conformation and bloodlines. The prices paid in these sales will reflect this. Sales later in the year and those that are not "select" may offer lower prices while still offering many possible champions. The yearling will need to be broken to saddle by your trainer. If all goes well, your yearling will be starting to race the following year at age two.

TWO-YEAR-OLD IN TRAINING. A "two-year-old" is a horse who has seen two birthdays on January 1. A two-year-old in training has already been broken and has had some training. This horse may sell for more than a yearling because of the breaking and training. These sales are usually held during the first six months of the year. At one of these sales you will have a better opportunity to watch the horse and check out its conformation. At this age, a trainer or owner may have a better idea of its athletic ability than when it's a yearling. Another advantage of buying a two-year-old is that the horse may be able to start racing right away. Some tracks begin racing two-year-olds as early as April. You might be able to receive a quick return on your investment. However, you must remember, two-year-olds are very young horses that are still growing and developing. They are subject to injury and bucked shins. Their knees and legs are still growing and changing. Many horses are not physically able to start as two-year-olds and may have to wait until they are three. Horses are not machines; they are flesh and blood. Two-year-olds will usually cost more than their younger counterparts because: (1) their physical conformation may be better defined; (2) the horse may be at a racetrack and showing a good way of moving; (3) the family's history for producing winners; and (4) workout times may be available on them.

Sex of a Horse

The sex of a horse really does not matter until resale or when the horse's racing career is ended, or if you wish to run in high stakes races, those that are gender-specific.

COLT. A colt is a male horse under the age of five who is capable of breeding (has not been gelded or altered). A colt will run in races listed for colts and geldings. At retirement, a colt who has a proven race record or excellent bloodlines can go into stallion service for breeding. Depending on his success at the track, breeders will pay a certain fee for the right to breed their mares to him. Once a colt turn five years old he is called a "horse."

GELDING. A gelding is a male horse who has been gelded or "fixed" so he is NOT capable of breeding. Gelding a horse is said to calm them down and they are sometimes easier to train because of it. They usually keep their mind on racing instead of breeding. A gelding will run in races with colts. At retirement, a gelding can be used for show jumping, hunter/ jumpers, dressage, and general trail/pleasure horses.

FILLY. A filly is a female horse under the age of five. Fillies are usually never altered and can produce throughout their lives. Fillies can run in races listed for fillies and mares as well as races listed for open company. At retirement, a filly can become a broodmare and start producing foals or they can become a jumper or pleasure horse. Once a filly turns five years old, she is then called a "mare."

RIDGELING. A ridgeling is a male horse with only one descended testicle. They are sometimes called a monorhid. They will run in races listed for colts and geldings. At retirement, they may or may not be able to breed. Like the gelding, a ridgeling can make a nice pleasure horse or jumper.

Owner/Breeder Incentives

STATE-BREDS. Owners and breeders can earn certain incentives, race for restricted purses and bonuses, by owning a state-bred horse. These incentives and bonuses can be distributed based on a percentage of a purse earned by a state-bred in a specific race. Funds may be given out annually according to a percentage of funds available and a sire's relative performance during that year. For more information on state-bred owner's incentives, contact the breeder's association for that state (see appendix). Many factors determine the amount and type of award paid including funds allocated, number of races for state-breds, and the size of the state's breeding industry.

STATE FOALED IN. Every sale catalog will indicate the state the foal was born or "foaled" in. Most states have specific races restricted to state-breds including high-value stakes races and owner incentives. State-bred restricted stakes races require nominations and sustaining payments from the year the horse is foaled until the race is run. For example, the state of Minnesota has eight restricted stakes races, six of which are for Minnesota Breds, the other two are for the progeny of stallions who donated and/or sold a season at the yearly Minnesota Thoroughbred Stallion Auction. While the state of birth means nothing on how the horse will perform, it will mean something if it is nominated to a specific stakes races in that state. Bloodlines of both the stallion and the dam are the important factors, not the state of birth.

STAKES ENGAGEMENTS. The bottom of each sales catalog page will list the stakes or breeder program races (e.g., Breeders' Cup, Minnesota Northern Lights Futurity, etc.). Being nominated and sustained makes the horses eligible to run in these races. They will have to meet the eligibility requirements to pass the starting gate at the time the race is run or may have to run in a trial. When purchasing a horse with nominations, it is important to remember that several sustaining payments may be necessary to remain eligible. These sustaining payments must be made by you, the owner. You are responsible to know when the payments are due and to make them on time. Some states will allow late payments with a penalty payment attached to it.

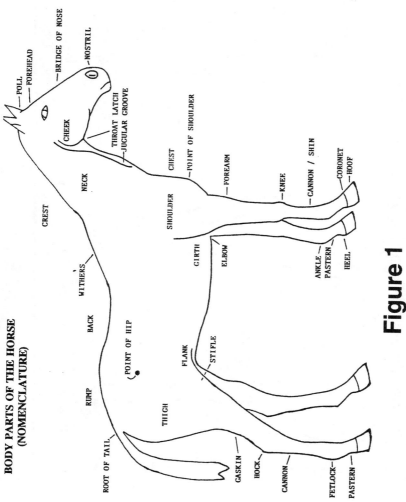

BODY PARTS OF THE HORSE
(NOMENCLATURE)

Figure 1

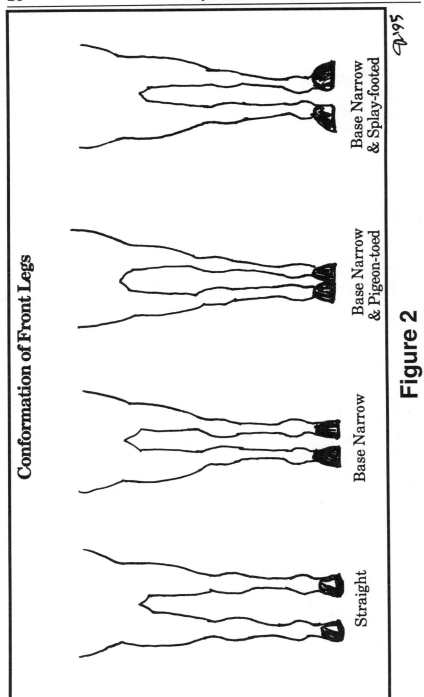

Conformation of Front Legs

Straight

Base Narrow

Base Narrow & Pigeon-toed

Base Narrow & Splay-footed

Figure 2

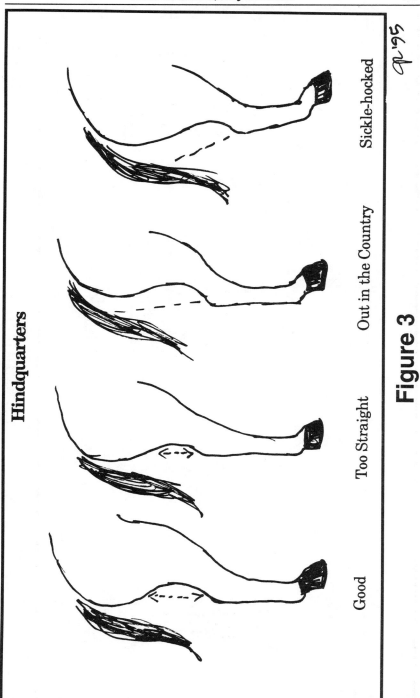

Figure 3

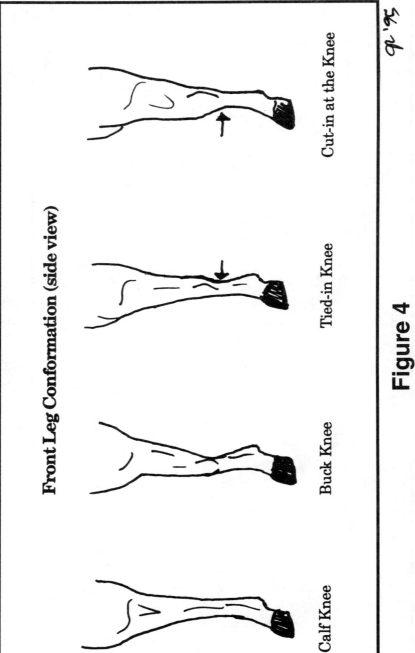

Front Leg Conformation (side view)

Calf Knee

Buck Knee

Tied-in Knee

Cut-in at the Knee

Figure 4

3

Hiring a Trainer

The most important aspect of owning a racehorse is hiring the right trainer. The future success of your horse business will depend a great deal on the trainer. This is the sole person to whom you are willing to entrust your horse. The trainer is the person who must transform your horse into an athlete without breaking him down. The trainer can act also as a qualified adviser. A good trainer should have an awareness of bloodlines and conformation. It is a good idea to have a trainer before going to a public auction because he/she can act as an adviser on the purchase of a horse.

There are no guarantees in finding the "perfect" trainer that is suitable to you. The following are some sound guidelines that have been used by successful owners to "hire" a trainer for their horse(s). Whomever you select should have a record which indicates that he knows his business. He should have a personality that is compatible with your own and there should be mutual respect and trust between you. No matter how well you follow these guidelines, there is one factor that you will need and that is good racing luck. Without good luck, the best horse can get into trouble and finish last.

Locating a Trainer

The names of trainers can be recommended or located in several different ways.

RACE TRACK STATISTICS. You can start with your local race track. Most tracks post a comprehensive listing of every trainer at the track. This listing contains the trainer's full name, number of starts at the meet, number of 1st, 2nd, and 3rd place finishes, in-the-money percentages, and total purse money earned. Take a serious look at the top 10 names on this list. These are the leading trainers at that track. Research their training statistics from reports that are available from bloodstock agencies.

RACING SECRETARY. Talk to the racing secretary at the track. Ask for recommendations of who you should talk to. The racing secretary knows who the best available trainers are at the track and should be able to suggest several names for you to contact.

RACING COMMISSION OFFICIALS. Trainers must take a lengthy set of written and oral tests and need to be licensed by the state racing commission. Check with the racing commission officials for any suggested names they might be able to provide.

OTHER OWNERS. Talk to other owners around the track. Ask them about their current trainer and past trainers. The list of the top money earning owners is posted at the track. Talk to those owners and find out what their trainers might be doing to get their horses into the money. If an owner had a bad experience with a trainer, find out what went wrong. Learning from someone else's mistakes and experiences can save you from making a mistake which could affect your horse.

Interviewing the Trainer

Once you have located a list of names, you now have the task of choosing which one is right for you. This sport is full of risk. There are many ways a racehorse can ruin itself, no matter how careful the training and handling has been. Give yourself the best chance to be successful by choosing a trainer that you can and have confidence in. If confidence is missing, the business relationship will not be successful for either of you.

ASK QUESTIONS. Interview the trainer and ask as many questions as you can to get to know his/her training style. You may have to interview and meet with as many as half a dozen trainers before you find the one that fits you. If a trainer is unable to answer questions or doesn't want to answer your questions, pass on that trainer. If the trainer won't answer your questions now, he/she might not answer them when your horse is in training either.

Questions should not just be one-sided. The trainer should be asking questions of you. He/she should be asking what you want. After all, during training you will want your trainer to be asking what you want your horse to be able to do. But remember, trainers are human and can't be expected to make a stakes winner out of every horse they train.

Ask questions to see if the trainer is knowledgeable and a dedicated horse person. Your trainer should be someone with a personality and philosophy compatible with your own. It is important to be able to discuss training approaches and methods for your horse and accept options and suggestions from your trainer. Ask how many horses the trainer has in his barn. You might want a trainer with a small barn (less than 10 horses) for more of the personal touch. Or you might not mind being in a barn with over 40 horses. However, many first-time owners can feel lost in a large barn.

AREA OF SPECIALTY. Question the trainer as to his/ her area of specialty. Some trainers prefer working with two-year-olds, fillies versus colts or geldings, claimers, three-year-olds, etc. Some trainers may not be able to work and break the two-year-old and might prefer older horses. Other trainers may excel in breaking the yearling and turning a two-year-old into a star. Some may specialize in routes (mile or longer) versus sprints (less than a mile), turf versus dirt. You have heard of "horses for courses." Training is no different with trainers than for horses. Find the trainer that will suit your horse and your ideals. Pay attention to trainers who claim horses and improve their performance. Trainers who have this ability should receive your consideration.

VISIT THEIR BARN/SHEDROW. It is extremely important to visit their barn and shedrow area on the backside. What you see there will tell you exactly how he/she will tend and take care of your horse. If the barn is not well-organized and orderly, the trainer may treat the details of training and conditioning of your horse in a similar manner. These are the important things to look for.

(1) How well are the stalls bedded? Little straw or sawdust means your horse may be subjected to bumps and bruises from sleeping on a hard surface. High bedding means comfort to your horse.

(2) Do the stalls contain plenty of fresh water? Are feed and water buckets kept clean?

(3) Is the shedrow swept and kept neat and tidy?

(4) What are the appearance of the other horses? Are their coats shiny and brushed or do they look like they haven't been brushed for a week?

(5) Is the tack room neat and orderly?

(6) What are the weights of the horses? Although racehorses are lean and muscular, showing some rib, are the horses

showing too much rib and appear to be underfed or fed poor quality of feed?

VISIT THE PADDOCK. Go to the race track and study the horses in the paddock. Watch for trainers who bring horses to the track looking fit and race ready. Watch also for trainers who bring over horses that have dull coats or lethargic appearances. Observing the horses in the paddock before a race is a good indication about the care the horse is receiving.

VANNING. Does the trainer own his/her own horse trailers allowing your horse to be vanned at a cheaper rate, or do they use a commercial vanning company? In either case, find out what the charges will be and what vanning company they use. If the trainer does use commercial vanning, it may cost more. Rates are based on mileage and the number of horses being transported. Find out if the vanning transport wraps the legs and makes frequent stops to give the horses a break. Vanning can be stressful to some horses. Because of your investment in your horse, be sure they are taken care of.

VETERINARIAN PREFERENCE. What vet do they use? What do they like about that vet? What are the potential costs for his/her services. Depending upon the health and/or any injuries of the horse, vet bills can range from $50-$1,000 per month or even higher. Find out how the trainer feels about pre-race medications such as lasix (medication for horses that bleed), bute (an anti-inflammatory pain relieving drug), or joint injections (cortisone). If the trainer is in favor of these medications, find out why he/she feels they are necessary. If you disagree about using these medications, make sure you have chosen a trainer who feels the same way. A vet bill showing a large amount of medications could be an indication that your horse is not well and should not be racing. Don't ever be afraid to ask questions about your veterinarian bill. Ask if you, as owner, will be consulted before any medications are given to the horse. Will you be contacted in case of an emergency illness or injury? As an owner, you have the right to make the decisions on the medication your horse should receive. You also have the right to refuse medication and give your horse a rest.

SHARE YOUR PHILOSOPHY. As an owner, you and your trainer should share philosophy on what you want to get out of owning a racehorse and the same how involved you want to be.

FULL OR HALF-YEAR CIRCUIT. Find out the entire circuit of a trainer. Where do they spend their summer and winter? Do they race year-round at several different tracks? If they do, what are the tracks. Do they have a place to board or lay up your horse wherever they go. If you choose to keep the horse in your home state, can the trainer recommend a good winter lay up to ensure the horse gets proper care until the next racing season? You may choose not to ship your horse to another track and not race him year-round.

SUCCESS RECORD. Find out from the trainer his/her past record of successful horses. Find out in what type of races the horses ran. What were their ages? Find out the distances and sex of the horses. Part of being a successful trainer is the ability to place their horses in the most appropriate race; race in which they can be most successful.

REFERENCES. Ask the trainer for a list of either past or current owners for whom he/she has trained. Talk to the owners and find out what they did or did not like about the trainer. Be sure and check out several people, because one person's dislike of a trainer does not mean the trainer is not good. However, if a trainer seems to lose owners faster than he gets new ones or does not want to give out a list of references, take that as a warning sign.

If a trainer's barn is full and they can't take on anymore horses, ask him/her to recommend another trainer.

Trainer's Fees and Charges

It is important to find out ahead of time the cost for what you will be charged for the trainer's services. This prevents any surprises or conflicts later. Arrangements may vary from trainer-to-trainer with owners; however, you will find the following to be fairly standard with most of them.

BREAKING FEES. These fees are for breaking a yearling or two-year-old to the saddle, bit, and reins. This is where the young horse learns to wear a saddle and have a rider on its back. This usually takes 60 days, and the rate averages $20.00 per day.

DAY RATE FOR TRAINING. These are the daily training fees charged to turn your horse into an athlete. This fee should include conditioning, galloping, breezing, working from the gate, feeding, watering, bedding, and bathing your horse. In the midwest, the average day rate will range from $25-$45 per day. In other regions, the average can range anywhere from $40-$100 per day.

LAYUP FEES. When a horse is resting in between racing meets or has become injured and needs to rest, they will require layup. Find out if the trainer has a facility where your horse can be cared for while he/she requires lay up. This fee is for the care and feeding of your horse until he/she is ready to go back into training. The fee is usually $10.00 per day. However, any vet care will be additional.

BONUS FEES. When your horse wins purse money (places 1st through 5th), it is usual and customary for a trainer to request 10% of your purse money as a "bonus" for getting your horse in the money. This is usually negotiated between trainer and owner when you hire him/her.

Checking Trainer's Record

Statistics are available though the Jockey Club on the past records of all trainers. The report is a performance report and is available to anyone for a fee. This service is available through owner's and breeder's associations who have access to the on-line Jockey Club or Bloodstock Research Information. It is a good idea to order the statistics on a trainer for a couple of years back. See how many starts their horse made and the number of wins and unplaced horses they have had. It is a good idea to check a couple of years' statistics because any trainer can have a bad year. Take a look at the average of the years.

Owner-Trainer Agreements

Many decisions made by you and the trainer will affect your horses productivity. Long-term decisions should not be made by your trainer alone. An informed owner should be involved in the decision-making. As an informed owner you should learn as much as you can about all aspects of your horse, including training and medical treatments.

Because your horse is an investment, it should be treated like any other investment and there should be a written agreement to protect it. It is important to develop the use of written contracts between owners and trainers that include specifics about medication, medical care, training fees, and lay ups for rest. These contracts could take care of any problems or questions that could come up later. These contracts could contain information on being consulted before medication is given to your horse, give you the option of taking your horse out of training to heal and rest, let a trainer know the limits he has in training, and the right to a second opinion for medical care. To protect you and your horse, consider "getting it in writing."

Hiring the Trainer

At long last you have selected your trainer. Sit down and discuss your investment in this venture and what you want to get out of it. You have made your decision, now give him/ her the opportunity to do what you hired him/her for--to train. Give them a chance to work with your horse, give them a season to train before judging their results too harshly. Changing trainers too often and continuously will not do your horse, nor your reputation as an owner any good. It is better to stick to one trainer long enough to see if he/she is making progress with your horse. However, if there are problems in communication and with the care of your horse, change trainers as you feel necessary. But, give them a chance first before you make the decision to either retain him/her or find another.

COMMUNICATION. It is the key to a successful relationship between you, your trainer, and success. It cannot be overemphasized enough. There must be two-way communication between both of you. The trainer should realize that the horse does not belong to him but to you. The trainer should inform you of your horse's progress, strengths, weaknesses, workouts, and injuries.

The trainer should be a professional. Only one person can train a horse. Questions of judgment on training should be left to the professional. However, this does not mean that the trainer should make all the decisions without discussing this with the owner. The owner should be able to be involved in the major decisions. Leave the conditioning to the trainer who does this for a living. He or she knows best the condition of your horse, how far it can run, how fast it can run, in what company it should run, and he/she should be able to pick a race for the horse. Remember, that is his/her job. However, if you do not understand something, don't be afraid to ask questions.

PRICE OF TRAINER. In all things, whether it is training, lay up, or breaking--you get what you pay for. Sometimes the cheaper fees might not be best. On the other hand, do not get a trainer who is so high priced that you will have difficulty paying him/her. If you want the best for your horse, check to see what the horse will be getting for the price. "Quality in" means "quality out." Remember, your trainer is performing a service for you and has monthly bills to make. Do your part as a good owner to pay your bills to him or her on a timely basis.

Together as a team--you can win at this game!

4

The Expenses of Ownership

Whichever form of ownership you choose, there are certain expenses that will be associated in owning a racehorse. Knowing what kind of expenses to expect will save you from being surprised later. In making a decision to own a racehorse, you should budget and plan for the "little" incidentals along the way. Before purchasing a horse, be sure that you understand what the projected expenses will be. Again, do not count on winnings to cover the expenses.

The Initial Investment

Your first expense will be in the purchase of the horse. The horse may be purchased at a public auction or privately from a breeding farm or individual. The price of the horse will vary depending on its sex, age, breeding, if it is nominated to any stakes races, and if it has had any training. No matter what the purchase price is, you will also be required to pay the state's sales tax, where applicable. If you are purchasing a horse in another state and shipping it to your home state, be sure and check out the state tax laws in that state as well. After completing the purchase of a horse, make sure you have the Certificate of Foal Registration in hand from the seller and check the description against the horse. This certificate should be given to you at no charge. Keep this Certificate in a safe place for you will need it to race or resell your horse.

Vanning/Shipping Expenses

Once a horse has been purchased you must provide transportation to get the horse home. If you do not own a farm or have the ability to care for the horse yourself, you will need to have him/her shipped to a boarding or training facility. Most public auctions will have commercial vanning companies available to transport your horse. The public auctions will require the horses to be moved from the sales area within 24 hours. Vanning costs will vary per company. The price is usually based on distance transported and can average from .35 to .40 cents per mile and on the number of horses being transported.

Vanning/shipping expenses should be added in your budget if you plan to ship from one racetrack to another even if your trainer will be doing the shipping.

COGGINS TEST. Before a horse can be shipped to a stable or track, a blood test must be done on the horse to insure that it does not have any infectious diseases that could be spread to other horses. This blood test is called the Coggins Test (equine infectious anemia) and is usually ordered by the trainer but is paid for by the owner. The cost is usually $20. EIA is a viral disease transmitted from an infected horse through blood transfusion and will remain in the white blood cells for life once the horse is infected. If you don't have a trainer at the time, you will be responsible to arrange for a vet to give your horse this test. The blood test is valid for one year and the vaccination certificate is attached directly to the horse's papers. The horse may then be shipped from track to track until the coggins certificate expires. You will also need a health certificate on the horse. Many states require a certificate even if your horse may be vanned through the state without stopping. It is a good idea to have a health certificate done by the vet when they are doing the Coggins Test. Health certificates are valid for only 10 days, so have one done on your horse just before shipping.

Layup/Boarding Expenses

When a horse is not in training or is injured, it needs to be boarded at a farm, stable, or other horse boarding facility. There is a daily charge associated with boarding which usually includes feed, bedding, indoor stall, and "outside turnout." The fee can range from $6.00 to $20.00 per day. Visit the farms and talk with the managers before sending your horse there. This fee does not include any veterinarian care (e.g., shots, worming, tests) or farrier expenses (shoes, trimming). There will be additional charges for these items. Remember, once the horse is purchased, he/she has to be fed every day!

Horse General Maintenance Expenses

The horse will require regular care whether in training or lay up and this will require visits from a veterinarian and a farrier.

VETERINARIAN. The horse will require booster shots usually in the spring and fall. These vaccinations are for Potomac Horse Fever, encephalomyelitis (sleeping sickness), strangles, influenza and rhinopneumonitis (commonly known as flu and rhino). The horse will also need to be periodically wormed either via paste or a tube method. If your horse requires such pre-race medication such as lasix (for bleeders) or bute (pain relieving drug equivalent to human aspirin), you will incur additional charges each time the horse races. Veterinary services can average between $50-$100 per month for a healthy horse at the track, considerably less for those on the farm. Supplemental veterinary care will be required should your horse become injured or sick. These costs can escalate depending on the type of care and if surgery is involved.

As an owner, you have the right to know what drugs you are paying for and why they are needed for your horse. Don't be afraid to ask. Some drugs may not be good for your horse over a long period of time. Do not allow your horse to receive drugs if a short period of rest will be better for him. Be in control of the types and quantities of drugs that are given to your horse. You are the owner and pay the bills. Do what is best for your horse.

A horse's teeth needs to be checked at least annually. A procedure called floating may need to be done. A horse does not have feeling in his teeth and floating is a procedure that files down the rough edges on his teeth. This procedure will keep the teeth in good condition to properly chew his food and aid digestion. Horses can also develop other dental problems similar to humans.

FARRIER. A farrier works with the horse's hooves by trimming and shoeing them. A horse's hoof is like a fingernail and grows constantly. The excess hoof must be trimmed frequently to prevent overgrowth. When in training and racing, a horse will require a new set of shoes every 4-6 weeks. A set of four shoes and trimming can cost between $50-$60. A simple trim can cost between $15-$20. Improper care of a horse's hooves can result in serious hoof damage and injury requiring veterinarian care. There is an old saying--no hoof, no horse.

Training Expenses

There are several different expenses associated with the training of your horse. Each expense is paid differently and at different times but are all related to training and need to be included in your budget. Don't expect your winnings to pay for training.

BREAKING COST. A yearling or two-year-old will require breaking to the saddle. This type of training is generally less expensive than when the horse is in training to be raced. Breaking is the method used by a trainer to "break" the youngster to wearing a saddle and to having someone on their back. This process can take anywhere from 60-90 days. Once this training has been successfully accomplished, the horse moves to the next level of training. The average cost for breaking can be from $15.00 to $20.00 per day.

TRAINING COST. Although racehorses are bred to run, it will require the patience and skill of a trainer to teach him/her how to do it. Training involves teaching the horse to gallop, change leads, how to rate and pace itself, make turns, and break from the gate. Like all athletes, the equine needs to be carefully conditioned. The horse is made fit and ready to win by the trainer. The trainer must also be skilled in interpreting a condition book to select the proper race for your horse. The average cost for training can range from $25 to $50 per day. Because the trainer plays such an important role in the career of your horse, selecting a trainer is just as important as selecting the horse. (See Chapter 3 - Hiring a Trainer).

PURSE STRUCTURE AND TRAINER'S BONUS. Each track has a different purse structure. Purses are the monies paid out to the top five horses. The purse for a race is divided by percentages based on order of finish. The usual distribution is 60%-1st, 20%-2nd, 11%-3rd, 6%-4th, and 3%-

5th. These percentages may vary by 1-2% from track to track. Recently, some tracks in Illinois and Minnesota are paying purse monies all the way down to last place. The percentage paid is usually 1% and is enough to pay at least the jockey's mount fee. Purse money varies between claiming, maiden, allowance, stakes, and added-money races.

In purchasing a horse, it is important to keep in mind the purse structure of the track you intend to race. Paying a large amount for a horse who may only race for purses of $5,000 will be a losing proposition because the horse will never be able to repay the original purchase price. Purse structures can range anywhere from $30,000-$180,000 per day. The purse structure allocated per day is spread between the 8-12 races that are run on that day. The higher the purse structure, the higher the money you will be able to win. The lower the purse structure, the lower the money you will be able to win. The purse structure of the track at which you plan to run should help determine how much you can afford to pay for a horse and still hope to break even or make a profit. Purses are determined by the "handle" which is the amount of money wagered that day at the race track. The higher the handle, the higher the purses. However, if the average handle goes down, the track may cut purses in the middle of a race season, or may raise purses if the handle increases.

If your horse finishes in one of the top five positions in a race (in the money), you will be awarded a percentage of the purse money based on in what position the horse finished. Once you are awarded this money, it is usual and customary that you will pay your trainer a bonus. The amount of the bonus is negotiated between the trainer and owner. Usually, the bonus is 10% of the purse money earned.

JOCKEY MOUNT FEES. In each race your horse will be ridden by a jockey. The trainer selects the jockey to ride your horse. The fee you pay for his/her riding services is called a jockey mount fee, and is based on amount of the purse of the race. Races with a purse value of $14,000 or less have fees ranging from $33-$45 per race. Races of $15,000 and up have fees of $50 or more. The fee is charged only on a losing mount. A losing mount is considered a horse who does not finish in one of the top three places of a race. If your horse finishes in one of the top three spots, the jockey mount is paid by percentage of purse money earned in the race. Usually, the percentages are as follows: 1st place - 10% of win purse, 2nd place - 5%, and 3rd place - 5%. These percentages may vary from track to track.

PONY/GATE FEE. All horses are taken to the gate by a pony rider. The pony rider takes your horse from a saddling enclosure, through the post parade in front of the grandstands, to the gate. The fee for this service is usually $10.00.

Stakes Race Expenses

Claiming, maiden, and allowance races will not require any entry fee other than a jockey mount. Some stakes races or graded races will require nominations and supplemental payments in order to enter. Generally, the higher the purse, the higher the nomination fee.

STATE ASSOCIATION STAKES RACES. States that have an owner's or breeder's association will sponsor races with high-value purses for their State-Bred horses. The State-Bred races usually are for two and three-year-old horses. A nomination is required when the horse is a weanling and sustaining nomination payments are made when the horse is a yearling and a two-year-old. To qualify to run in the race, your horse may only have had to won a certain amount of money or have run in a futurity or derby trial to qualify.

If your horse qualifies to "pass the gate" in one of these races, you may be required to pay an additional amount to start the horse. These fees are in addition to the jockey and gate fees. "Passing the gate" is the terminology used by the Racing Secretary to indicate that your horse has qualified to enter and run in the race.

Licensing Expenses

All states require you to have a valid owners license issued by the state racing commission. If you race in more than one state, you will be required to have an owner's license for each state. Each member of a partnership or syndicate owning 5% or more of the horse, must be licensed also. A license usually costs $25-$30 each. The license should be applied for or already issued BEFORE your horse races. The license will entitle you to race your horse(s), claim other horses, get into the track free, park free, and gain access to the backside of the track.

The state racing commission will also require you to be fingerprinted. Your fingerprints are sent in to the FBI for a background check and the charge for this is usually $30.

Jockey Silks Expense

The origin of individual racing silks (colors) began in October 1762 in Newmarket, England, with the kings racing each other. The Jockey Club came up with the idea of using individual silks to help distinguish the horses that were running and to prevent disputes from not knowing the colors worn by each rider. They had an agreement to have the colors attached to the horse worn by their respective riders. The Stewards then asked the owner to take care that the riders be provided with clothing accordingly. In other words, to purchase the riding "silks."

Back then only nineteen owners were listed with registered colors. Today there are over 19,000 registered racing silks with a variety of designs. It is no longer necessary to register your silks with the Jockey Club, however, it is a good idea to choose a pattern that is unique and not similar to another owner's silks. Selecting your silks is a personal matter and you will want to choose a color and design that fits with your own personal preference.

If you own the horse by yourself, it will be necessary for you to purchase and design your own racing silks. If you are in a partnership, the managing partner may use their silks or sometimes a partnership will collectively design silks for just that partnership. The silks are worn by the jockey riding your horse that day. The silks are kept in the jockey's room and washed after each race. There are two kinds of racing silks: traditional and aero-dynamic.

TRADITIONAL. Traditional silks are made of nylon, are loose fitting, and they do not fit tight to the body. Sometimes they "balloon up" in a wind as the jockey is coming down the stretch. Jockeys prefer this kind if they are wearing the new flak jacket protector vest. Flak jackets are a protective vest worn by the jockeys to prevent injury if they are thrown from a horse.

AERO-DYNAMIC. Several years ago, a new form of silks were created; aero-dynamic silks. These were close fitting silks and believed to cut down on wind resistance to help increase a horse's time. The material used is lycra and is similar to the material used for diving wetsuits. It has not been proven to cut down the running times. Jockeys who wear the flak jacket protector vest find these types of silks to be tight and uncomfortable. They also are more expensive. Purchase of either the traditional or the aero-dynamic type silks is strictly a personal decision.

DESIGN. You can choose from a large number of colors and designs. Most racing silks today use a combination of diamonds, blocks, bars, stripes, circles, and chevrons. The more complicated the design, the more expense involved. Usually traditional racing silks will cost approximately $100. The aero-dynamic silks may run from $150-$250. Helmet covers can be made for an extra cost but are not necessary.

Equine Insurance Expenses

When purchasing a horse, you may want to consider buying insurance on the horse. The cost of insurance policies will vary and can change from year to year, actual amounts or percentages cannot be quoted with any degree of accuracy. If you are considering purchasing a policy or policies, check with an insurance agency selling equine insurance to get accurate prices. There are various types of policies available. They are:

MORTALITY. This insures the horse for its assessed value or purchase price if it should die. This is normally purchased if a large sum of money was paid for the horse. If the horse is a colt or stallion, this insurance could protect your interest in its breeding career should it die before he "is put out to stud."

THIRD PARTY LIABILITY. This is standard insurance and is fairly economical. This type of coverage protects you against any third party claims which may result from bodily injury or property damage caused by your horse at the track or boarding facility (e.g., horse breaking loose in the paddock and striking a fan). The HBPA (Horsemen's Benevolence and Protective Agency) offers a third party liability insurance to all licensed owners at a very nominal cost and is available through other insurance companies as well.

WORKER'S COMPENSATION. This insurance covers the jockeys and exercise riders who ride the horse and covers them in case of an accident or injury while riding the horse. Most trainers are required to carry this coverage before they are allowed to train at a track. It is important to find out if your trainer has this coverage. If your trainer does not, it is highly advisable that you take out a policy to protect yourself or ask yourself how responsible your trainer's policies are?

5

The World of Racing

Once you enter the world of racing, you will meet many people and officials aside from your trainer. All of these people have important roles to play with you, your horse, and the racing industry. Becoming an informed owner can help increase your potential to be successful. There are many rules and regulations in horse racing. You have certain rights as an owner and breaking these rules could subject you to fines and penalties. Not knowing your rights could lead to mistakes that could have been corrected by speaking up at the right time. This chapter will introduce you to the people found on the backside working with your horse, and to the racing officials who have jurisdiction over the rules of racing.

The Backside

Most of the activity involving your horse will occur in the stable area or "backside" of the track. The backside is a world of its own with its own language and culture. As an owner you should become familiar with the backside to ensure that your horse is being cared for in a healthy environment. This is where he trains to become an athlete. His stall is located here. The trainer or groom will bathe, feed, and care for him. As an owner you will want to come out in the morning to watch your horse gallop or breeze in a workout.

The backside should not be confused with the frontside of the race track. The frontside is where the grandstand, club house, and betting tellers are located. This is where the races are run. The frontside contains a saddling enclosure, walking ring area, and main track. This is where your horse will go when he is ready to race, and where the patrons place their bets on the races.

You will also want to become a part of your local horsemen's organization, Horsemen's Benevolence and Protective Association (HBPA). The HBPA is a horsemen's group formed to help horsemen. They are also involved in negotiations with the track on purses and number of racing days. They also can assist you in obtaining low cost third party liability insurance for your horse. A good owner should be an informed and active member of their horsemen's group because it is involved in important decisions concerning you and your horse.

EXERCISE RIDER. Trainers hire an exercise rider to gallop and exercise your horse in the morning. An exercise rider will usually gallop the horse once or twice around the track based on the trainer's instruction. The trainer is responsible to pay the exercise rider for his services.

PONY HORSES. Sometimes a trainer may decide to exercise a horse with a "pony horse." To "pony a horse" means that a pony rider will take the horse on a lead rope at the side of the pony. The racehorse does not carry any weight but will run alongside the pony horse. On race day, a pony horse will take the racehorse to the gate. Because racehorses become very excited, the pony will accompany the horse and jockey and his presence helps control the racehorse until he enters the starting gate.

JOCKEY. The jockey is hired by your trainer to ride your horse in a race. Jockeys are experienced in knowing where to be when riding a horse and good ones can give a horse the desire to run. Sometimes a jockey can lose a race with a moment of bad judgment. Good luck plays a part in each race. A jockey can make all the right decisions, position your horse well, and then get taken out of a race by a horse bumping or colliding into your horse. Jockeys are all trying their best to win. Your trainer will try to find the best available jockey to ride your horse. You may wish to suggest certain jockeys to your trainer or suggest one of the top jockeys. However, top jockeys at a track can pick and choose their mounts and are more than likely to pick one they think can win because their income is in direct relationship to their performance. Don't be upset at them or your trainer if they do not choose your horse. If your trainer gives specific instructions to a jockey and they don't follow his orders, the trainer may choose to change jockeys next time, As an owner, you will be paying the jockey mount fee for him/her to ride your horse. If the horse finishes in the top 3, the jockey is entitled to a percentage of the purse money as well. The jockey may exercise your horse in the morning. A trainer will try to get the race jockey to also ride him during timed workouts.

JOCKEY AGENT. The jockey agent works for the jockey and acts as a middle-man between the jockey and the trainer. It is the jockey agent's responsibility to get riders for his/her jockey. Since the agent receives a percentage, usually 25%, of the jockey's earnings, he will be trying to get the best horses. The agent will approach your trainer to have his jockey ride your horse. Sometimes the trainer will approach the agent. Agents have the authority to enter your horse in a race for the trainer. You, as the owner, also have the authority to enter your horse if your trainer cannot do so. The jockey for your horse must be named at the time of entry. If the same jockey is named on two different horses in the same race, it is up to the agent to select one of the two horses. Another jockey will either be named or assigned to your horse.

VALET. The valet takes care of a jockey's equipment. He makes sure the correct silks are pulled for the race and that the proper weight is in the lead pad of the saddle. The lead pad is a section of the saddle where lead is inserted for proper weight assigned to the horse. In each race, horses are assigned to carry a certain amount of weight based on their age, sex, and number of wins. The valet brings out the saddle and saddlecloth and helps the trainer saddle the horse. After the race, he meets the jockey on the track and carries the saddle and equipment back to the jockey's room. He makes sure the equipment is cleaned and ready for the next race.

Racing Officials

There are many rules and regulations in horse racing supervised by state commissions. As an owner, you need to be aware of the rules because breaking them could subject you to fines and penalties. The racing officials also assist in keeping racing fair and honest. It is important to know your rights as well as the regulations.

RACING SECRETARY. The racing secretary has the most difficult job at the track. This is the person who writes the "condition book" and is directly responsible for the horses running in each race at the track. He must "write" races he thinks can be filled by the horses at the track and may come in conflict with trainers who want other races written. The racing secretary is employed by the track and also has the responsibility to the betting public to provide the best "race cards." He can contribute to the success or failure of a race meeting by the races he writes. The racing secretary can be found in the racing office located on the backside. The racing office is where the trainers file ownership papers, enter horses and handle the business of racing. Stall applications are sent to him and he decides which horses will be stabled on the backside.

STATE/TRACK VETERINARIANS. The track veterinarian makes pre-race examination of all entered horses the morning of each racing day to ensure the sound racing condition of the horses. Horses that are sore, lame, or sick may be scratched by the veterinarian. During the post parade, at the starting gate, during and after the race, the track veterinarian is observing them for any signs of unsoundness or bleeding. The state veterinarian is in charge of the sample urine collections taken from the winners of each race. They also certify "bleeders" to be put on lasix, a drug that aids in preventing bleeding. A bleeder is a horse who bleeds from either the nose or into the lungs and this is not always evidenced without an examination. If a horse is sick or scratched, it is placed on a "vet's list." A horse cannot be removed from the vet's list until it is examined and certified healthy by the track veterinarian.

PADDOCK JUDGE. Before the race, all horses are saddled in a paddock or saddling enclosure under the supervision of a paddock judge who will check lip tatoos and the markings of each horse. He verifies any equipment changes such as blinkers. He gives the orders to lead the horses out, calls the riders up, and out to the post parade.

STEWARDS. The stewards are to racing what an umpire is to baseball. Their most visible action to the public is in declaring each race as official. They also have the ability to put up the inquiry sign if they think a foul has been committed during the running of a race. The stewards are located high above the track and have a commanding view of the race. There are several cameras mounted at different angles around the track and the stewards have contact with patrol judges stationed at different points around the track as well. During each race, the Stewards watch for any possible foul, whether intentional or accidental. Riders must keep their horses running in a straightforward path and cannot move in front of other horses without sufficient clearance.

The Stewards settle disputes in races if a jockey lodges an objection against another jockey. They must review and judge the incident. If no foul has been committed, the original finish of the race will stand. If a foul has been committed, the guilty horse will be dropped lower in order of finish. Jockeys, trainers, and owners have the right to lodge a claim of foul to the stewards after the race. If a race has been declared official, the trainer or owner has 24-48 hours to lodge a "protest" on the outcome of the race. A "protest" requests a further review of an incident or action. Purse money will be held until the Stewards have time to further review the race. Once a final decision is made, horses may be disqualified and placed lower than original finish or remain the same. Purse money will then be released.

The stewards also oversee the conduct of all licensed personnel on the track including owners. If licensed personnel are found guilty of breaking a rule, they can be fined and/or lose their license.

PATROL JUDGES. The patrol judges are positioned around the track and assist the stewards in reporting any interference or foul occurring during a race. They are also responsible to call in jockeys involved in questionable incidents. They may suspend a jockey as a result of their observations.

STARTER. The starter is in charge of the starting gate and oversees the horses once they leave the walking ring or saddling enclosure. He is responsible for ensuring a fair start after seeing that all horses are facing forward and standing on all four feet. The assistant starters lead the horses into the gate and hold their heads straight. Before a horse makes its first start, it must "break" from the gate several times. After they demonstrate the ability to do this properly, the starter will certify them "gate approved."

CLERK OF THE SCALES. The Clerk of the Scales is in charge of the jockey's room. He weighs each jockey before and after the race to ensure that the jockey has carried the required weight. The Clerk also reports all over-weights to the announcer and stewards. The assistant Clerk of the Scales is usually in charge of the silks room. This is where all of the owner's silks are kept. At the end of each day, the Clerk files a report that goes to the Horsemen's Bookkeeper for distribution of purse money and jockey fees earned.

HORSEMEN'S BOOKKEEPER. The Horsemen's Bookkeeper transacts business with owners and trainers. All entry fees and jockey mounts are required in advance and need to be deposited with the Bookkeeper. Each owner needs to have an open account when you have a horse. The Bookkeeper also becomes the paymaster and pays out purse money earned. Purse money is usually held in the account for 3-4 days until the winning horse's drug test clears. Once the money is released, it can be drawn out. The Bookkeeper also accepts money from owners and trainers when they put in a claim for a horse. All owners should ensure that the Bookkeeper has current address and tax identification information. If owners do not keep their account current and owe money for jockey mounts, the Bookkeeper reserves the right to hold horse's registration papers until the fees are paid in full.

STATE RACING COMMISSIONS. Each state racing commission has authority over the conduct of racing and management of the track. By state law, a commission is appointed by the governor to regulate the conduct of racing. They regulate the number of days, approve purse schedules, and oversee the conduct of all personnel at the track. The Commission licenses all owners, trainers, jockeys, and track personnel and oversees the testing of horses for drugs after each race. The commission employs an administrative staff to handle day-to-day affairs throughout the year.

6

Is Ownership Right for You?

The crowning moment of owning a racehorse is when the gates spring open and your horse comes bounding out and gives it his all. He gives 110% regardless of whether he wins or loses. But you need to be aware that statistics indicate that only 5% of racehorse owners make a profit. It is difficult to make a profit with racehorses. About 40,000 foals are registered with the Jockey Club each year and from that number, only 6% will ever win a race. This sport is a gamble and a risk. It comes with no promises and is filled with many disappointments.

We all want the "derby horse" right away and when that doesn't happen, there is great disappointment. You must face the reality that few horses will justify their cost. Do not be caught in the illusion that every horse will begin training, win many races, and earn big money right away; not every horse that starts training will make it to the track. This makes the joy of owning a horse that does win, the experience of a lifetime. If you are ready to accept the disappointments along with the triumphs, then you are ready to become a race-horse owner.

This is a sport that grows on you and you will begin to love it. As you become more involved in your horse, you will grow to be a part of it. Once you own a racehorse, your life will never be the same. People will tell you over and over, not to become too attached to your horse and that it is a business. This does not stop you from caring and loving them--unless you end up with a barn full of pets. A horse knows when his owner cares about him, and will run for you. It does not hurt the racing industry to have more individuals in it who have feelings and who care about the horses. Because of the low percentage for profit, many people own a racehorse because they love the spirit of the horse and love the sport of racing.

This book contains the basics that you need to know to get you started in owning a racehorse. It is not all inclusive and there will be other things you will need to learn along the way. Experience is the best teacher and learning can be fun. Hopefully, with the information given in this booklet, that experience will become a rewarding and a winning one.

The horse is an interesting, alluring animal and if we choose to play in this game of chance, tomorrow may be the day when we hit the derby horse. Tomorrow may be the day when everything turns out all right. Because there's always another horse, another chance, another hope, another tomorrow, and another race. Don't quit. Find confidence within your heart and strive ever harder toward your dream, and you won't be denied.

Rules in Ownership

There are several important rules to follow in owning a racehorse. They are summarized as follows.

EDUCATE YOURSELF. Education leads to success. Learn everything you can about the conformation and selection of a racehorse. Refuse to buy a "cheap" horse if that's his only virtue. Know your limitations. Don't buy until you become knowledgeable or can locate a trustworthy advisor.

Teach your advisor on how to communicate with you and talk honestly with him. Learn about the economics and expenses of owning a racehorse. Don't expect any winnings to pay for the expenses. Be honest with yourself as to how much you can afford to spend. Read all that you can find related to the racing industry. Subscribe to industry-related magazines. Attend seminars and join owner/breeder associations.

SEEK OUT ADVICE. Finding a competent advisor is one of the important decisions you will make. Find an experienced horse owner, trainer, or consultant who possesses knowledge, demonstrates competence, and has a personality compatible with your own. Ask questions of other owners and trainers.

GO SLOW. This is a complex business that can't be learned in a few months. If you find a good advisor, try to keep him/her as you develop your business plan and purchase a horse. Start out slow with one horse or maybe join a partnership. A good thing about partnerships is that each partner can combine their monetary resources to purchase a better racing prospect and share in the expenses. Group ownership can also foster new friendships which can make racing more fun. Ask yourself how many horses you can afford to buy and pay expenses. Don't go overboard and buy too many horses, causing you to go into debt and create a bad image of racing. Ask yourself if you can afford to own a racehorse.

BUSINESS PLAN. Develop a written business plan, plotting out where you want to be three or four years down the road, and how you want to get there. Time goes faster than you think. Don't put off writing your plan. Devote your energies to developing a winning strategy.

QUALITY HORSE. It is better to own a percentage of a good horse than to own all of a poor horse. Look for the best quality that you can afford. Don't expect a graded stakes winner the first time out. Look for a horse that will be able to make it to the track and run. The stakes horse will come in time. When he does come it will have been well worth the wait.

BE PATIENT; PAY YOUR DUES. Be patient. You will make mistakes. Your first horse may not win but that is part of paying your dues in the industry. The enjoyment of owning a good horse (or a great one) is worth pursuing. It's what makes dreams come true. All good things come to those who wait.

Affordability Worksheet

Here is your chance to evaluate how much you can afford to spend on owning a racehorse. The following worksheet includes most of the usual and customary expenses to be expected in purchasing and training a horse. The worksheet is just a general outline and you can modify it to suit your own needs. In some of the areas I have provided an estimated average amount that is charged for the expense/service. If you find this amount to be higher or lower in your area feel free to adjust this amount. After all, this is your worksheet. When you have finished the worksheet, total all the expenses. The total may amaze you. If you are seeking a partnership calculate the percentage you wish to own. You can then see if you can afford 100% of a horse or only a percentage. This worksheet is only a guide. You will have to make the final decision.

Purchase of a horse:
    Yearling
        $_____ + $_____ sales tax =   _____
    2-year-old
        $_____ + $_____ sales tax =   _____
    Claimer
        $_____ + $_____ sales tax =   _____
    Bloodstock Agent Fees
        Cost of Horse $_____ x 5% =   _____

Shipping Expenses:
    From auction
        $_____ x _____ miles =   _____
    To Trainer/Race Track
        $_____ x _____ miles =   _____

Miscellaneous Expenses:
    Racing Silks
        Aero-$\_\_\_\_\_ or Traditional-$_____ =
    Owner's License
        $30 x _____ # tracks =   _____
    Equine Insurance
        $_____ (will vary) =   _____
    Tatoo Expense
        $50 x _____ # horses =   _____

Veterinarian Expenses:
    Coggins Test
        $20 x _____ per year =   _____
    Worming
        $20 x _____ each =   _____
    Health Shots
        $40 x _____ each =   _____
    Monthly Rate at Track
        $100 x _____ months =   _____

Farrier Expenses:
   Trimming
      $15 x _____months =   _____
   Shoes
      $55 x _____ months =   _____

Boarding/Layup Expenses:
   Board at Stable
      $10 x _____ days =   _____

Training Expenses:
   Breaking
      $20 x _____ days x _____ months =_____
   Day Rate
      $45 x _____ days x _____ months =_____

Nomination Expenses (if any):

   Sustaining Stakes Payments Due

      $_____=   _____

Grand Total (estimated) =   _____
Percentage for partnership =   x _____%
   (must be greater than 5%)
My Liability for 1 year = $_____

The Winner's Circle

The purpose of this book is to educate and encourage racehorse ownership, if even only a part of one. Owning a racehorse can be the high of a lifetime if approached realistically as to the expenses. If handled properly, the enjoyment you will get out of the racing experience will far exceed the cost to you. The enjoyment goes well beyond the winning. The enjoyment will take you into the world of the racehorse and touch you. You'll never be the same after being touched by one of these magnificent animals. They are truly an equine athlete of the highest standards. It is a thrill that can't be equalled. If it's right for you, the winner's circle is the place to be.

If I have helped even one person achieve their dream of owning all or part of a racehorse or have enlightened you to the "other side" of the race track, then this book has been worth all the time and effort put into it. My job is done and yours has just begun.

Focus your energy

and the commitment will carry you

to your dreams.

AFTERWORD

I wrote "Derby Dreams" out of a sincere desire to help people, like yourself, pursue the dream to own a racehorse. My intention was to write a comprehensive book outlining all aspects of the business including expenses and what you can expect in return. I have tried to provide you with information about the racing business that will enable you to stay the course, be prepared for the emotional highs and lows, and be an asset to this great industry.

I have shared my victories and disappointments in the hopes of starting you down the right path. Learning is a never-ending process. With every horse and with every year in the business, knowledge deepens, and I wish to revise this book accordingly. I would be delighted to hear from you, the readers, so that your comments and experiences may be included in future revisions. Tell me which chapters were helpful. Offer your suggestions for improvement. Let me know what areas still perplex and puzzle you or what new chapters you would like to see. Tell me what you didn't like about the book or which chapters may be too vague and need further clarification. Send your letters and ideas to me in care of the publisher's address below. I encourage you to write and help me make this book better. By writing, you will be making it better for yourself and all others who wish to pursue the dream.

Although I have researched all sources to ensure accuracy and completeness of the information contained in this book, as author, I assume no responsibility for errors, inaccuracies, or omissions. Any slights against people or organizations are unintentional. Readers should consult an attorney or accountant, where appropriate, for specific applications to your individual racing needs.

Best of luck!

Derby Dreams
Dark Horse Publishing Co.
P.O. Box 322
Rosemount, MN 55068

APPENDIX
Organizations & Information Sources

This list is not all inclusive. There are more associations throughout the United States. However, they chose not to be listed.

CALIFORNIA THOROUGHBRED BREEDERS ASSOCIATION
Attn: Nathaniel Wess
P.O. Box 60018
Arcadia, CA 91006-0018
In addition to membership, they publish a monthly magazine, Thoroughbred of California.

**FLORIDA THOROUGHBRED BREEDERS' &
OWNERS' ASSOCIATION**
Attn: Richard E. Hanrock
4727 NW 80th Avenue
Ocala, FL 34482-2098
In addition to membership, they publish a bimonthly newsletter, F.T.B.O.A. Newsline/Hotline.

IDAHO THOROUGHBRED BREEDER'S ASSOCIATION
Attn: Dianna K. Timm
5000 Chinden Boulevard, Suite E
Boise, ID 83714
In addition to membership, they publish a monthly magazine, Idaho Hoofbeats. Telephone Number: (208) 375-5930, FAX (208) 375-5959.

**ILLINOIS THOROUGHBRED BREEDERS' &
OWNERS' FOUNDATION**
Attn: Pat Whitworth
P.O. Box 336
Caseyville, IL 62232-0336

IOWA THOROUGHBRED BREEDERS & OWNER ASSOCIATION
Attn: Vicki A. Janssen
798 43rd Avenue
Prole, IA 50229
In addition to membership, they publish a monthly newsletter. Telephone number: (515) 981-5283.

KANSAS THOROUGHBRED ASSOCIATION
Attn: George Smith
P.O. Box 35
Medicine Lodge, KS 67104

OHIO THOROUGHBRED BREEDERS & OWNERS ASSOCIATION
Attn: Gayle A. Babst
920 Race Street, Suite 201
Cincinnati, OH 45202
In addition to membership, they publish a bimonthly magazine, Ohio Thoroughbred, stallion register, and stakes schedule/farm brochure.

KENTUCKY THOROUGHBRED ASSOCIATION/
KENTUCKY THOROUGHBRED OWNERS & BREEDERS INC.
Attn: David L. Switzer
P.O. Box 4158
Lexington, KY 40544

MICHIGAN THOROUGHBRED OWNERS &
BREEDERS ASSOCIATION
Attn: Sue
P.O. Box 2752
Livonia, MI 48151
In addition to membership, they publish a monthly magazine, The Michigan Thoroughbred. Telephone number: (313) 422-2044.

MINNESOTA THOROUGHBRED ASSOCIATION
P.O. Box 508
Shakopee, MN 55379-0508
In addition to membership, they publish a bi-monthly newsletter.

NORTH CAROLINA THOROUGHBRED ASSOCIATION
Attn: Beth Muirhead
4312 Carlisle Road
Hillsborough, NC 27278
In addition to membership, they publish a magazine Midatlantic Thoroughbred.

NORTH DAKOTA THOROUGHBRED ASSOCIATION
P.O. Box 2496
Bismarck, ND 58502
In addition to membership, they publish a bimonthly newsletter, Keeping You Informed.

NEW YORK STATE THOROUGHBRED BREEDING & DEVELOPMENT FUND
575 Lexington Avenue, Suite 2605
New York, NY 10022

In addition to membership, they have an incentive program to encourage breeding of thoroughbreds in New York.

OKLAHOMA THOROUGHBRED ASSOCIATION
Attn: Gary D. Simpson
100 NW 63rd, Suite 200
Oklahoma City, OK 73116

In addition to membership, they publish 10 times yearly the magazine, The Homestretch, and annual stallion register; conduct stakes races, including Oklahoma Classics Day; and are horsemen's representative at Blue Ribbon Downs.

OREGON THOROUGHBRED BREEDERS ASSOCIATION
Attn: Ursula V. Gibbons
P.O. Box 17248
Portland, OR 97217-0248

In addition to membership, they publish a bimonthly magazine, Washington Thoroughbred with Oregon Horse published as a section of it.

TENNESSEE THOROUGHBRED OWNERS & BREEDERS ASSOCIATION
Attn: Matt Hamilton
P.O. Box 158504
Nashville, TN 37215

In addition to membership, they publish a newsletter, TTOBA Newsletter.

TEXAS THOROUGHBRED BREEDERS ASSOCIATION
Attn: Ed Dodwell, President
P.O. Box 14967
Austin, TX 78761

In addition to membership, they publish a monthly magazine, The Texas Thoroughbred. Telephone number: (512) 458-6133, FAX (512) 453-5919.

THOROUGHBRED OWNERS AND BREEDERS ASSOCIATION (TOBA)

Attn: John Y. Hamilton, Executive Director
P.O. Box 4367
Lexington, KY 40544

In addition to membership, they publish a monthly magazine, The Blood Horse, and hold owner seminars. Membership includes many benefits, please contact for more information. President: Helen C. Alexander; Vice President: Ronald Kirk; and Vice President: John Ed Anthony. Telephone number: (606) 276-2291, FAX (606) 276-2462.

WASHINGTON THOROUGHBRED BREEDERS' ASSOCIATION

Attn: Ralph Vacea, General Manager
P.O. Box 88258
Seattle, WA 98138

In addition to membership, they publish a monthly magazine, The Washington Thoroughbred, have breeders' awards, have available research libraries and on-line computer, video library, THRUST Scholarship Program, and sponsors educational programs.

Newsletter

BACKYARD RACE HORSE

3708 Crystal Beach Road
Winter Haven, FL 33880

This is a newsletter dedicated to the pleasure and joy of the race-horse. The purpose is for networking for owners and trainers and educating them and give them tools for defending yourself in the industry. This newsletter is produced by Janet Del Castillo, author of Backyard Race Horse.

Public Auction Contacts

While there are many state auctions, the following is a list of the major national sales contacts. For information on any state auctions, contact the state owner and breeder association.

KEENELAND SALES

P.O. Box 1690
Lexington, KY 40592-1690
(606) 254-3412

OCALA BREEDERS' SALE CO.

P.O. Box 99
Ocala, FL 34478
(904) 237-2154

FASIG—TIPTON THOROUGHBRED AUCTIONS
2400 Newtown Pike
Lexington, KY 40583-3610
(606) 255-1555

Equine Book Sellers

Many hard-to-find books on equine information can be found through one of the following mail-order companies.

BREAK THROUGH PUBLICATIONS
P.O. Box 594
Millwood, NY 10546-9989

EQUINE RESEARCH INC.
P.O. Box 535547
Grand Prairie, TX 75053

HUSBAND COMMUNICATIONS
P.O. Box 801503
Santa Clarita, CA 91380-1503

THE RUSSELL MEERDINK COMPANY, LTD.
1555 South Park Avenue
Neenah, WI 56956

Magazines

Both of these magazines are issued weekly:

THB BLOOD HORSE
P.O. Box 4038
Lexington, KY 40544-4038

THE THOROUGHBRED TIMES
P.O. Box 420235
Palm Coast, FL 32142-0235

This magazine is issued monthly:

THE BACKSTRETCH
19899 W. Nine Mile Road
Southfield, Michigan 48075

BIBLIOGRAPHY/ RECOMMENDED READING

BREEDING

BREEDING MANAGEMENT & FOAL DEVELOPMENT, by Equine Research
>Covers every possible topic on breeding and foaling a horse.

BUSINESS PLANS

DEVELOPING A BUSINESS PLAN FOR AN EQUINE OPERATION, by Barbara Ann O'Kelly
>Easy to read, easy to use, fifty-one pages of text on equine business and questionnaires and forms. By the end of completing the exercises and questions in the book, the reader will have your own custom business plan. (Available from Husband Communications.)

CONFORMATION

CONFORMATION EVALUATION, by Dr. Dewitt Owen
>This 75 minute video gives you an excellent understanding of conformation. The video is far better than a book because you will actually see all conformation defects on real horses.

SPECIFICATIONS FOR SPEED IN THE RACEHORSE: THE AIR-FLOW FACTORS, by Dr. Robert Cook
>Dr. Cook details the importance of good airflow in racehorses and how to select a horse with good airflow conformation.

OWNERSHIP

BACKYARD RACE HORSE: THE TRAINING MANUAL, by Janet Del Castillo
>Prediction Publications & Productions, 3708 Crystal Beach Road, Winter Haven, FL 33880; 1992. This book will guide you through training a horse away from the racetrack and how to form a sound racehorse. It also gives an honest presentation of the realities of owning a racehorse and provides an excellent overview of what to expect when you join the world of racing. Available through the publisher above. A must-read for all new owners.

SUCCESSFUL THOROUGHBRED INVESTMENT IN A CHANGING MARKET, by Jack Lohman & Arnold Kirpatrick
The authors advise you on how to select an advisor, costs of the horse business, what to buy and avoid at sales, and much more.

HORSEWATCHING, by Desmond Morris
An excellent book on horse's expressions, body language, and social behavior.

TRAITS OF A WINNER - THE FORMULA FOR DEVELOPING THOROUGHBRED RACEHORSES, by Carl Nafzger
Nafzger gained international attention after he guided an unknown young colt named Unbridled to win the Kentucky Derby and the Breeders' Cup Classic. He is one of racing's most respected trainers and has a knack for getting the most out of every horse. Here are his thoughts, philosophy, and wisdom from a man at the top of his game. It's a book for owners wanting to learn more about managing their thoroughbred investments.

THE BODY LANGUAGE OF HORSES, by Bonnie Ledbetter
Reveals the nature of equine needs, wishes and emotions, and how horses communicate them.

THE COMPLETE GUIDE TO CLAIMING THOROUGHBREDS: FINDING, FIXING & MAKING WINNERS, by Tom Ivers
Here are some strategies to use to identify horses that can be claimed and outlines ways to make the ownership of claimers a profitable adventure.

TAXES

HORSE OPERATIONS MANUAL, by Kenneth Wood
Business and tax tools for the horsemen. Provides suggestions and examples to assist you in setting up a management plan and recordkeeping.

OWNERS & BREEDERS TAX MANUAL, by Thomas A. Davis
An authoritative treatise on federal taxation of horsemen. Broad coverage includes expense deductions, depreciation and employment taxes. (Available from the American Horse Council or Husband Communications.)

GLOSSARY

A

ALPHA: The strong, dominant foal who is the leader of a group of foals.

ASSISTANT STARTER: The track employees who lead horses into the gate and handles the horses while in the gate until the start is given .

B

BACKSIDE: The stable area of a race track.

BIT: A metal bar in the horse's mouth to which reins are attached by which the horse is guided and controlled.

BLINKERS: Eye cups attached to a hood to limit a horse's side vision and prevent distraction.

BLACK TYPE: Boldface type used in sales catalogues to show horses who have won or placed in a stakes race.

BLOODLINE: A horse's pedigree showing the dam and sire and their race record.

BLOODSTOCK AGENT: A broker who represents an owner/buyer in the purchase of a horse at a public auction, in exchange for a commission.

BREEZING: Running during a morning workout with the rider exercising some restraint on the horse.

BROODMARE: A mare producing foals.

BUSINESS PLAN: A written plan outlining where you want to be in three or four years.

BUTE: A horse medication allowed in many racing jurisdictions that is used to control inflammation. It is similar to aspirin.

C

CALF KNEE: Where the knee of the horse is set back from the cannon bone.

CLAIMING RACE: A race for horses that are eligible to be purchased for a specified price by a licensed owner.

CLERK OF SCALES: A racing official whose responsibility is to check the weight of all jockeys before and after the race.

CLOCKER: Person employed by the track who times workouts in the morning .

COGGINS TEST: A blood test done on a horse to insure that it does not have any infectious diseases.

COLT: A male horse under the age of five who has not been castrated or gelded.

CONDITION BOOK: A booklet written by the racing secretary every two weeks listing all races, conditions, and other information on the race meet.

CONFORMATION: A horse's basic physical appearance.

CONSIGNOR: The person who is selling a horse at a public auction.

CORPORATION: A legal entity operating under a grant of authority from a state in the form of articles of incorporation.

D

DAM: The mother of a horse.

DAY RATE: The rate charged by a trainer to train a racehorse.

DERBY: A stakes race exclusively for three-year-olds.

E

EXERCISE RIDER: A rider who exercises horses in the morning during training hours.

F

FARRIER: A blacksmith who does the shoeing and trimming of horses.

FILLY: A female horse under the age of three.

FOAL-SHARING: An agreement between a mare owner and a stallion season owner to share a foal.

G

GALLOP: A morning workout when a horse is running from slow to moderately fast, but not as fast as a horse runs when he is working out.

GELDING: A male horse of any age who has been altered or castrated.

GROOM: A stable employee, employed by the trainer, who grooms and cares for the horses on the backside.

H

HOMEBRED: A horse bred and raced by his owner.

HORSE: A male horse five years or older who has not been altered or castrated and capable of breeding. Also known as a stallion.

HORSEMEN'S BOOKKEEPER: The bookkeeper transacts business with owners and trainers and is the paymaster of purse money.

J

JOCKEY: A professional rider who rides racehorses for a living.

JOCKEY AGENT: A person employed by a jockey to secure riding mounts in a race.

JOINT VENTURE: A commercial undertaking by two or more persons to the completion of a single project (co-ownership).

L

LASIX: A horse medication allowed in many racing jurisdictions that is used to control bleeding in a horse from respiratory exertion.

LEAD PAD: A piece of equipment under the saddle in which thin pieces of lead may be inserted to bring a jockey's weight up to the assigned weight for a specific race.

LEAD PONY: A horse used to lead the racehorses from the paddock to the starting gate.

LIMITED PARTNERSHIP: Similar to a regular partnership except each limited partner contributes their share of money to a managing partner and have limited liability for the partnership.

M

MAIDEN: A horse that has never won a race.

MARE: A female horse four years of age or older.

O

OVER AT THE KNEE: Where the knee of the horse is over from the cannon bone (the reverse of calf knee).

P

PADDOCK: The area where the horses are saddled and viewed prior to a race.

PADDOCK JUDGE: The racing official responsible for getting the jockeys and horses from the paddock to the gate and is responsible to check the equipment of each horse.

PARTNERSHIP: A partnership is the relationship existing between two or more persons.

PATROL JUDGE: A person employed by the track to assist the stewards in viewing the running of a race to watch for infractions and fouls.

PEDIGREE: The bloodline of a horse.

PIGEON TOED: Where both front hooves of the horse point inward.

PURSE: The amount of money distributed to a designated number of finishers in a race.

R

RACING SECRETARY: The official who writes the conditions for the races, receives entries, and is responsible for the operation of the race office.

REGISTRATION CERTIFICATE: The document forwarded by The Jockey Club that certifies the horse as a duly registered horse along with all identification markings, registration number, owner, breeder, state foaled, and past race win record, if any.

RESTRICTED RACE: A race restricted to certain starters because of their place of birth or previous winnings.

RIDGELING: A male horse with only one descended testicle.

S

SIRE: The father of a horse.

SHEDROW: Stable area with barns and walkways under a roof.

SILKS: An owner's chosen colors and designs worn by the jockey while riding the owner's horse.

SOLE PROPRIETOR: The simplest form of a business organization. Apart from you, the owner, the business has no existence.

SPLAY FOOTED: Where the hooves of the horse both point outward.

STALLION: An entire male horse capable of breeding to mares.

STALLION SEASON: The right to breed one mare to a particular stallion for one specified season.

STARTER: A track employee who is in charge of the starting gate and insuring a fair start for all horses.

STATE-BRED: A horse bred and/or foaled in a particular state making it eligible to compete in special races or for purse supplements.

STEWARD: Racetrack official that presides over the race meeting, rules on claims of foul or any protests, imposes fines and suspensions.

SYNDICATE: A syndicate is the public sale of the multiple interest in a horse.

T

TATTOO: A form of identification in which racehorses are marked under the upper lip with a letter/number combination from their registration certificate.

TRACK VETERINARIAN: The veterinarian who makes pre-race inspections in the morning of all horses racing each day.

TRAINER: The person who conditions and prepares horses for racing.

V

VALET: An employee who takes care of a jockey's equipment, carries the saddle and equipment to the paddock, helps the trainer in saddling the horse and meets the rider after the race to carry the equipment back to the jockey's room.

VANNING: Commercial transport of horses that charge by the mile.

W

WEANLING: A foal after it has been weaned from its dam to the time it becomes a yearling on January 1st following its foaling.

WINNER'S CIRCLE: The enclosure adjacent to the racing oval where a winning horse is brought for a win photo with the owner, trainer, and friends.

WORKOUT: A training effort usually done in the morning in which an official time is recorded by the clockers and published in the program.

Y

YEARLING: A horse between the first New Year's Day after being foaled to the following January 1.

INDEX

80

ABOUT THE AUTHOR

Mary Lou Reeb Werner is a native of Bismarck, North Dakota, now residing in St. Paul, Minnesota. She is employed by a federal government agency, is a Certified Professional Secretary, has an Associate of Applied Science degree in Business from Normandale Community College.

She became a racing fan in 1986 and joined her first partnership in a racehorse in 1988. Since then, she has experienced several different forms of horse ownership including sole owner, limited and general partnerships, and was manager of a joint venture. In 1994 she started a breeding operation in Arizona. She has raced thoroughbreds at Canterbury Downs in Minnesota, Fonner Park and Aksarben in Nebraska, and Turf Paradise in Arizona.

A member of the Minnesota Thoroughbred Association (MTA) since 1989, she has been very active serving on the Race and Breeders Fund Committee, Stallion Auction Committee, and Education Committee. In 1994 she was elected to the Board of Directors of the MTA and currently serves as Chairman of the Education Committee.

She has also been active in the Horsemen's Benevolent and Protective Association (HBPA) serving on the By-Laws and Constitution and Election Committees. She is also a member of the Arizona Thoroughbred Association.

Well known at Canterbury Downs, now Canterbury Park, in Minnesota as a Racing Ambassador volunteering her time and services at Canterbury and county fair events introducing many people to the Sport of Kings. She staffed a new owner's booth at Canterbury and during a "Fill the Downs" promotion brought 330 new people to the track. She was also an active volunteer in 1994 on the Off-Track Betting amendment campaign in Minnesota.

Her writing career began in 1992 when she wrote the booklet, "So You Want to Own a Racehorse," which was published by the MTA. She was the guest speaker at a new owner's seminar held at the Canterbury Inn in August 1992. She has also published an article in the April 1995 issue of PC Laptop Computers magazine on how she uses a laptop computer to handicap the races and keep records on her equine operation.

Her interests include cake decorating, ceramics, writing, and her horses - retired and racing.

To order additional copies of **Derby Dreams,** complete the information below.

Ship to: (please print)

Name _____

Address _____

City, State, Zip _____

Day phone _____

_____ copies of *Derby Dreams* @ $9.00 each $_____

Postage and handling @ $3.00 per book $_____

Minnesota residents add 6.5% tax $_____

Total amount enclosed $_____

*Make checks payable to **Dark Horse Publishing***

Send to: Dark Horse Publishing
P.O. Box 322 • Rosemount, MN 55068

- -

To order additional copies of **Derby Dreams,** complete the information below.

Ship to: (please print)

Name _____

Address _____

City, State, Zip _____

Day phone _____

_____ copies of *Derby Dreams* @ $9.00 each $_____

Postage and handling @ $3.00 per book $_____

Minnesota residents add 6.5% tax $_____

Total amount enclosed $_____

*Make checks payable to **Dark Horse Publishing***

Send to: Dark Horse Publishing
P.O. Box 322 • Rosemount, MN 55068